TEACHING/DISCIPLINE

CHARLES H. MADSEN, JR.
CLIFFORD K. MADSEN
The Florida State University

Allyn and Bacon, Inc.
Boston

Teaching/Discipline

BEHAVIORAL PRINCIPLES
TOWARD A
POSITIVE APPROACH

Printed in the United States of America

Library of Congress Catalog Card Number: 76–85379

Second printing . . . May, 1970

To our parents—lifelong teachers,
unwitting behaviorists,
wonderful people

CONTENTS

INTRODUCTION

This book is written especially for the teacher and prospective teacher. It is intended as a teacher's guide in the use of behavioral principles relating to classroom discipline and subject-matter presentation. The text is presented in three parts. Part I is organized in question-answer schemata designed to help clarify the central issues that have arisen from the authors' interaction with children and teachers in the public schools. Part II represents a selected summary of scientific and professional practices deemed relevant, transferable, and directly applicable to classroom teaching. Part III treats the effect of teacher responses on student behavior.

It has been the intent of the authors to present this material without excessive technical terminology. We assume that involved terminology is not warranted in an introductory text and initially offer only the Greek ἀπολογιὰ to explain the manner by which we disregard, oversimplify, redefine, and generally abuse classical antecedents in order to effect communication with the teacher. We are deeply indebted to the researchers whose studies are summarized as Scientific Applications in Part II and more specifically to their unnamed scientific progenitors. We are hopeful that this short work will not only stimulate the beginning of greater efficiency in the classroom but will also provide an impetus for teachers to take fuller advantage of the benefits being produced through scientific research.

PART I

Teaching and Discipline

TEACHING

The Art of Discipline

A first day?

As she approached the school, she wondered why all schools look the same. Why couldn't someone be imaginative enough to disguise the telltale landscape and those separate rows of windows that indicate the time-honored concept of individual classrooms? Why were all the buildings that didn't look as though they were designed by school boards called experimental? What about those experimental programs, anyway? Were there communities that really cared enough about education to pay for all that? It was obvious this wasn't one of them. Notice the dull color of the paint; that quonset hut must be new, but what a poor excuse for an education site. Oh yes, that must be a "portable classroom"—a nice euphemism for lack of planning or no money. Money—this job didn't pay that well. Why was she here? Parkside had a better program, or perhaps she should have stayed in school. The graduate assistantship could have come through, and why even teaching? But, then, why think about all that nonsense anyway? This is the day, the first day for the students. She felt her stomach skip and her throat tighten. Was it this bad for everyone? As she walked into the building she wondered why those other people looked so calm? She stopped at the restroom. Wasn't this the third time since getting up this morning? Her eye caught a limerick, and she wondered why students were not as creative in class as they were on bathroom walls. Why were all these wild thoughts so vivid this morning? "Okay, face it—you're scared. Just plain scared!"

Her mind wandered back to a discussion with her father. There was a teacher—fifty years in the public schools. She had gone home especially to talk to him those two weeks before the planning session. She remembered her father smiling as she asked him many questions. She remembered getting no answer day after day until the last evening before she was to leave. "But Dad, what makes a good teacher?" After a long silence his brow furrowed, and his bright eyes narrowed.

"Every teacher goes out with a golden apple of knowledge he wants to share, but some students don't want that knowledge, and their attitude becomes, 'Teach me if you can, but I'll make it as difficult as possible.' Remember two things. When it is as difficult as it can be, don't give up. You might think that it can't get worse, but it does when you give up. The second thing—*you can't even get started without discipline.*" As she looked in the mirror after washing her hands, she became suddenly angry with her father and that discussion. Clichés, clichés, that's all she needed now—two more clichés: "Don't give up. Discipline." She remembered her professors—more clichés. "Motivate the students, captivate their interests, recognize individual differences." Great, great, but how? No one ever says how. As she approached her room, she felt guilty about her thoughts concerning her father. Sure, he *was* a fine teacher—years of compliments, awards, letters, everything a teacher could want. Then she suddenly realized that even her father didn't know why. The art of teaching—is it really that elusive?

When she got to the door, she stopped for a long moment. "Please, please let me be a good teacher." Then it happened. The door knocked against her face as a student ran out. She watched the boy run down the hall as the students inside started laughing. She wondered quickly if she should go after him. "No, I'd better stay with the class." She had rehearsed an opening joke; that wouldn't work now. She felt her face flush as she tried to decide what to do. After a long pause she muttered, "Good morning," but instantly realized that it was a mistake when one boy softly mimicked her. Again, laughter. Why, oh why couldn't she start all over again? She looked over the sea of faces. Where was a friend? She quickly picked up a piece of chalk and began writing her name on the board. With her back turned, she tried frantically to think of some way to gain control. She heard some small noises, then a girl's louder voice, "Quit it." Was it this way everywhere? From kindergarten through twelfth grade, was this what teaching was all about? Finally she spoke. "Students, please take your seats so we can get started. As you notice on the board, my name is . . ." Two boys were standing in the back. "Would you please take a seat?" The class turned around to see. One boy shrugged "OK, OK, OK." The class burst out laughing again as he dropped into a chair. The other boy started to move, but then stopped as the class laughed louder. "Would you please sit down!" The class grew quiet. She felt her heart pounding and mustered the sternest look she could. Student and teacher were now staring at each other. The classroom became not only quiet but also electric as students looked from teacher to troublemaker and back again. After these thousand years of silence, she heard herself say angrily, "Now, you sit down this instant." Nausea came into her stomach as she watched the muscles tighten in his face, his lips curl sarcastically. "Are you goin' to make me?" **A first day?—A large majority of teachers who leave the teaching profession do so because of what they term "inability to discipline."**

Whom do we discipline?

Many teachers and parents have drawn an artificial line between love and discipline. Some make a point for love; others for discipline. The wise think they solve the problem when they say it must be both, and all are perhaps equally naïve. The most essential point is that we as teachers must understand precisely what we mean by love and/or discipline before we can begin. The major thesis of this book is that we must be concerned with how people *act* in order to assess behavior or to define terms. How should one know that he is loved but by the way people act toward him: what they say, how they look, how they touch, in a word, what they *do?* Attention, praise, spoken niceties, and physical contact have been demonstrations of love for years. Who cares if someone loves them if they never receive evidence through attention, contact, or the spoken word? While it may be possible for love to exist in total abstraction, most people are not content with such little personal involvement, especially over an extended period of time. One often hears the phrase "I'll love you no matter what." This is a good example of a meaningless cliché. Indeed very few, if any, really believe it. "No matter what" remains an abstraction that has little meaning until it is violated. That is, I'll love you until you desert me, find someone else, treat me cruelly, violate my trust, and so on. Most people do stress overt behaviors. A more fitting phrase would be, "I'll love you if you love me," or "I will act in certain ways with you if you reciprocate."

If such statements as "I will love you no matter what" were left to idle verbalizations, there would be little problem. When they are taken seriously, they pose a very serious problem, especially for the teacher. The teacher is led to believe that teachers should "love" everyone; and, if this were not damaging enough, the teacher actually may believe that one should continuously *act* as though one loves all students "no matter what."

One behavioral principle which we try to teach all youngsters is simple. "When you do nice things, nice things happen to you. When you do bad things, bad things happen to you." Even allowing for slight inconsistency, if we truly believed and taught in a manner conducive to this end, we would shortly have many "nice children." Yet we violate this principle regularly by teaching a child the exact opposite. This simple principle has several perversions: (1) when you do *bad* things, *nice* things happen to you; (2) when you do *nice* things, *bad* things happen to you; (3) no matter what you do, *bad* things happen to you; and (4) no matter what you do, *nice* things happen to you (i.e., I'll love you no matter what). Perhaps the saddest ramification of this last distortion is that while we treat the child, for a time, as though all behavior deserves nice consequences, we finally give up on the child at that precise point when he has finally learned exactly what we have taught him: No matter what he does, nice things happen to him. We often crown this educational achievement with statements such as: "I've tried everything with that child and nothing works," or "I just can't get through to that student."

Discipline is a process whereby certain relationships (associations) are established. It is a way of behaving, conducive to productive ends. First, it must be taught; secondly, it must be learned, i.e., internalized. Love, if it is to transcend mere rhetoric, is a way of feeling and acting conducive to productive ends. Most teachers enter the teaching profession because they truly love children (care about students) and desire to help each child achieve his greatest potential. Sometimes, people are paid to care about children, i.e., to teach.

The most difficult aspect of human interaction based upon love is to develop the ability to withhold overt acts of love (ignore or disapprove) to help the child learn appropriate ways to behave. When love responses have been previously established, we can then respond in similar kind to the child's behavior. Thus, when a child demonstrates inappropriate responses and we actively withdraw our overt responses of love, we teach the child that his behavior is not deserving of love responses from us. The most tragic mistakes of the teacher occur when the courage to act in this way is absent, and the teacher succumbs to "giving in." The child learns a perverted association: "When I do bad things, nice things happen to me." In the long run everyone suffers, but mostly the child. The authors call this teaching behavior "mistakes of love." More appropriately it might be classified as "naiveté" or "lack of courage." It is amazing, although apparent, that some people actually believe that all responses should be regarded with overt acts of love. The teacher who really loves a child will have the courage to teach him proper associations. We discipline only those people we care about; others we leave alone. **Whom do we discipline?—We discipline those we love.**

Why do we discipline?

Discipline is necessary if a child is to function properly. All teachers have had the unfortunate experience of observing either children or adults who are "undisciplined." We usually refer to such people as lacking motivation, apathetic, rowdy, or even mean, spiteful, or deceitful. But why are children so classified? How do they become this way? If self-discipline is to be internalized, then how is the child to achieve this attribute? The answer is obvious—*it must be learned.* Teachers often "beg the question" by stating that it must come from *within* the child. Yet how does motivation or proper attitude get "in"? Even if some of it is "in," will it continue to serve in the future? These are questions with which the teacher must deal.

Particular patterns of responses are leaned from the external world (external stimuli). If a student is "motivated," it is because he has learned to associate certain behaviors with certain outcomes. Motivation does not exist in a vacuum; it is a way of behaving. If the teacher wants a student to behave in a certain way, the teacher must structure the student's external world (i.e., control his environment) to insure the desired outcome. The disciplined child is a child who (1) has learned to behave socially in appropriate ways, and (2) evidences proper patterns of responses to academic work. If either one of these two general categories of behaviors is absent, we usually say the child "has a problem."

We must be very careful, however, not to designate many behaviors into one artificial category and believe we have solved the

problem because we have arbitrarily classified it. People react differently
to various situations (stimuli). It is very interesting to take a pencil and
paper and write down one's own responses in different situations. How
do we act in the classroom, in church, at a football game, in faculty
meetings, swimming, buying shoes, driving a car, getting out of an
invitation, giving a speech, eating dinner, listening to beautiful music,
listening to an argument? Yes, we act differently, we dress differently,
we talk differently, we even smile differently in these diverse situations.
If we were brave enough to list our most secret behaviors, we would
probably shock those very people who believe they know us the best. It
is unwise to classify behaviors into artificial categories that have to do
with only a few situations. Perhaps some justification can be made for
general attributes (e.g., apathetic, aggressive, boisterous, unmotivated),
but such classification is extremely deceptive and at best provides only
partial information.

Specificity is the key to behavioral analysis, and the teacher must
deal with each specific situation in order to teach proper associations. In
academic work most teachers would not begin to classify children into
all-inclusive categories. Because Mary is excellent in spelling does not
mean that she is exceptional in geography. Similarly, because she does
not constantly disrupt the class does not necessarily indicate that she is
"well behaved." Is it not curious that when referring to social skills we
tend toward greater classification with much less justification considering
the magnitude of individual responses to social stimuli?

In our complex communication, we have developed a certain
"shorthand" for descriptive purposes. Words such as love, motivation,
discipline are used as though these words had meaning apart from
specific situations. It would be extremely difficult "to communicate"
without using such a short-word system. However, we should remember
that each situation is different. Every particular word refers to many
different behaviors, and each association merits specific consideration.
When speaking of discipline we must specify the nature of the situation
and the response. When we use the word as an abstraction referring to
many separate behaviors, we must realize that definitions of discipline
must be specific to certain behaviors if the teaching of proper associations is to take place.

How, then, are we to get the student to learn the many behaviors
that will provide him with the necessary skills to achieve a productive

life? Within the complexity of his many responses to his external environment, we must structure his external world to provide proper relationships to be learned. We should not sit back and hope that motivation will somehow "get inside." We must structure the environ-ment to provide the student with proper associations. Discipline must first be external; it must come from *without* before it can be from "within.")

If learned relationships to external stimuli are conducive to productive ends, the child will have a repertoire of responses that will serve him well as he meets the constant challenges of life. If he is capable of following rules, acting enthusiastically regarding new learning experiences, staying on task during work periods, relating well with other children, knowing when to be assertive and when to acquiesce, indeed, if the student has learned to respond appropriately to many specific situations, then we say he is well disciplined. **Why do we dis-cipline?—We discipline to provide for social order and individual pro-ductivity.**)

What does discipline take?

The late President Kennedy in his book *Profiles in Courage* stated the problems of the politician in facing the demands of continued popularity as opposed to acting on the courage of his convictions. Politicians are not alone in this dilemma. Few people realize the pressures placed upon the teacher for conformity and popularity. This pressure comes not only from community, administration, and parents but from colleagues and students as well. It is much easier to go along, to not rock the boat, to reevaluate one's position, especially in relationship to "touchy problems." It *is* difficult to discipline the principal's daughter, to face the disapproval of a colleague, or to face an irate parent who insists his child has been dealt with "unfairly." It is difficult to explain a simple behavioral approach which rests on direct immediate consequences and not on intriguing deceptions. It is difficult to explain to a parent that *the question of discipline is not one of strictness or permissiveness but one of cause-and-effect relationships.* It is difficult to show parents how they can help their child when the teacher's instructions to parents require opposite parent/child inter-actions than those previously established. It is difficult to live through the first day of a new program in discipline without giving in. It is *most* difficult to lose, for a time, the favorable response of a child.

Any teacher is faced with the problem of wanting to be liked. In our society being liked is an admirable goal. It is indeed easy to demand a little less, hoping to be liked. Some people's desire to be liked is so great they will suffer mild contempt for the privilege. Furthermore, most teachers come to realize that even the most sophisticated students often evaluate a teacher's worth in terms of entertainment: "Here I am; what do you have for me today?" The value of discipline is not likely to be cherished immediately. Regardless, it should be remembered that the *teacher's approval* is probably much more important to the student than vice versa. The teacher's personal approval is one of the teacher's most effective rewards. *It should not be given indiscriminately.* Indeed, one never does a person a favor by letting him get away with anything, especially that which he does not like about himself. If the teacher really knows in what he believes, he is must less likely to succumb to pressures. **What does discipline take?—It takes courage.**

2

DISCIPLINE

The Way to Learning

What do students bring?

At any time in the chronological development of a child, we are prone to look back into the child's history to explain his present behavior. Thus, we have a never-ending spiral which assesses blame backwards (behavioral antecedents). Colleges blame the public schools, public schools blame the home, and the parents blame each other or the child's progenitors *ad infinitum.* If we must stop somewhere, let us stop at birth, although some theoreticians would input motives even before the child's first breath.

Let us consider three oversimplified, but rather characteristic, views of the child at birth: (1) the child is born good, (2) the child is born bad, and (3) the child is born neither good nor bad. If, as some believe, all children are born basically good, then the child's only impairment is the corruption of living. The teacher's goal would be not to corrupt his basic nature. This would not be difficult in a Utopian world. Perhaps it would not be difficult in the world in which we live, if all behavioral responses were predestined to be ideal. A problem arises, however, when "good" is specifically defined; each person's idea of the "good" does not always coincide with another's. A second problem arises for the teacher if the child has somehow been previously corrupted, for now the child evidences both "good" and "bad" behavior.

The second view proposes that children are born bad. In this case the teacher's job would be to correct the basic "badness" so the child could be "good." Again we have a problem with definition of "bad," especially without reference to specific overt behaviors. It is curious that many people who believe in this "badness" theory assume quite readily that childrens' good behavior is *not* learned, but that all that bad behavior (usually referring to moral transgressions) must be eliminated. Regardless, if the child has learned any "goodness" at all, he will still present a mixture of both "good" and "bad."

The third position postulates neither good natures nor bad and, therefore, assumes that all behavior is learned. The teacher's job in this situation simply would be to teach the child correct responses. Nevertheless, in all probability the child will have picked up some "bad" behaviors. Therefore the same situation will be evidenced as with the other two positions. The important question regarding the foregoing is: What should the teacher do? Regardless of philosophical orientation, should the teacher's responses to the student be any different? Indeed, *is it possible to start teaching at any other place than where the student is?* Suzy, Sam, and Fred all cry out in class—Susy because her sweet nature has become corrupted, Sam because he was born bad, and Fred because he learned some wrong associations. Does it really matter what their personal history or the teacher's philosophy has been? The important question would seem to be: What does the teacher do? Even if we could solve the philosophical problem or know the particular individual reinforcement history of the individual children, they are still crying.

All too often we pretend we have solved a problem because we can find some explanation for the behavior (e.g., high score on "problem child tests," family depravity, "bad seed," terrible 1st-grade teacher). Unfortunately, the children will continue to cry out in class until we do something to change their behavior. During the very first processes of interacting with the child, the teacher should be able to find out just *where the student is both socially and academically.* These first encounters with the student provide all that is needed to determine where the student is. The teacher can then begin to do something concerning the student's behavior. An involved analysis by the teacher is generally both unproductive and unnecessary.   **What do the students bring?—It does not matter.**

Who has the responsibility?

Teacher X has a problem child. In almost every situation when he should be acting one way, he is acting another. His behavior gets constantly worse in the classroom until the teacher can take it no longer. The teacher passes the point of feeling frustrated and, if honest, will admit strong dislike toward this source of constant harassment. The teacher decides to find out just what the student's problem is. The student is sent to the school counselor; and, after an extensive battery of tests, social reports, and time-consuming investigation, the teacher gets an answer: "Johnny is a problem child." On every one of the "problem child tests" (personality scales), he scored extremely high. Not only did all the tests indicate that he was indeed a problem boy (exhibited deviant associations), but the report concerning his home life was even worse. Teacher X cannot help feeling pity when learning of his terrible home situation and begins to wonder how he survived as well as he did. Teacher X discusses his home situation with a close colleague, and both of them marvel anew how bad life for some children can actually be. Johnny continues to be a problem child, but now his teachers *"know why"* (high test scores—bad home). He will probably not finish public school; he will probably grow continually harassing society and end up in other more stigmatized institutions. "How tragic, but what can a teacher do with a home situation like that?" Obviously nothing—the end?

Man is a complex organism. Among his many attributes is an ability for exceptional discrimination. All of his empirical senses provide a basis for remarkable differentiation. At an early age (approximately six months) he can even discriminate between people. He learns what to touch, what not to touch; he learns a complex language system; he learns auditory and visual discriminations; he learns to yell at playtime and to sit quietly during individual study periods. He even learns to "put on" a teacher if he can get away with it.

Of course Johnny is a "problem child." That is precisely why he was sent to the counselor. And how unfortunate it is that there are many "diagnosticians" whose major purpose is merely to confirm the prognosis of the teacher—if their terminology can be understood. Johnny will continue to be a problem child until someone teaches him different responses. He has learned a repertoire of responses to deal with his world—the more antisocial his home environment, the more deviant will be his responses.

The truly pathetic situation is that no one will *teach* Johnny. The one place where there is some hope for Johnny is the school. Yet many teachers quickly abdicate responsibility once his history is known. *Johnny can discriminate.* He can be taught new responses to deal with that other world outside the home. He can learn to read, write, spell; he can learn new rules of social interaction and thereby break the cycle of his past. If cooperation is impossible, he can even learn these responses *in spite of a bad home.*

It is not easy to deal with the Johnnies. They take time, energy, and a disciplined teacher. All the Johnnies do not even survive; yet for these children, *the school is their only hope.* **Who has the responsibility of discipline?—The teacher.**

Why don't they learn?

Many questions have been raised in relationship to why Johnny doesn't learn. Often the proponents of these questions do not support their queries with long-term constructive encouragement. Instead, scathing indictments are directed toward those very teachers who spend a great deal more time worrying about why Johnny doesn't learn than do most of their critics. In every aspect of learning, continued educational research is needed to ascertain and remediate learning difficulties. Yet at present the teacher must strive to do the best job possible.

Education is stressed in many ways in our culture. Quite naturally we often assume that everyone wants to learn. We even assume that they want to learn what we want them to learn. Some children do not want to learn. Others do not want to learn what we think they should learn. The reaction of the teacher should not be amazed bewilderment (the teacher's reinforcement history includes values established through sixteen years of learning) but a basic question: *Why should they want to learn?* Children must be taught to be motivated, curious, or interested, i.e., to establish their own goals. Some children are just too comfortable to learn. Why should one learn to speak, let alone properly, if all desires are met without this particular mode of verbal symbolization? Why should one learn a difficult mathematical system if gazing out the window passes the time better? Why should one practice spelling if one finds that more attention is received when one wanders around the room, or writes a "special note," or plays at the pencil sharpener, or does any number of more fun things than spelling?

The desire to learn must be taught. Appropriate learning behaviors must be established that provide some **reward**. No thinking adult wastes time in idle pursuits that are difficult and meaningless. How can the teacher expect everyone automatically to want to learn, especially when it may represent work? **Why don't they learn?**—Because the rewards of learning have not been established.

What if it's work?

Most people assume the responsibility of work. We speak often about work: working on a project, going to work, getting work, finishing our work, and so on. In education we often speak about school work; yet we have a burgeoning conspiracy to turn work into play. Most teachers realize the importance of making work as palatable as possible. If students get excited about work they consider it play, and everyone is much happier. The ingenious teacher has striven for years to turn work tasks into play. The great teachers are those who are able to elicit a pleasurable response toward the most rigorous pursuits.

Unfortunately, our highly technological society has turned many work tasks into play without a corresponding discipline toward those tasks that are still "work-work" tasks as opposed to "play-work" tasks. The young boy's delight in finally building his very own plane wanes appreciably when confronted with a common battery-propelled toy that flies instantly and can be purchased for a fraction of his allowance. Most adults will testify with pride to those endeavors which represented, for them, true discipline. Patience, repetition, and arduous industry are still required for long-term achievement and happiness in almost every activity of life. Yet we have more and more "instant avenues to success." The problem for today's teacher is not only in structuring "play-work" (technology is providing wonderful aids in this regard), but in teaching the necessary discipline for *long-term* rewards as well (i.e., establishing maturity). If behaviors conducive to long-term goals are not acquired early, it is much less likely they will be acquired later on.

Today's schools provide many extracurricular activities with almost as much turnover as there are activities. The possibilities for diverse activities become greater and greater for the growing child. Almost all his time can be spent changing from one activity to another. Consider specialized fields such as music, art, and creative writing. How many times have we said as adults, "I'd give anything to play like that, or to paint like that, or to write like that"? Of course we would *not.* We know what it would take in time and effort. The irony is not that some do not have any such skills; it is that they do not have enough understanding concerning processes of acquisition to appreciate the skill evidenced in others.

This should not indicate that the teacher should take pride in being a punishing taskmaster. It is extremely unlikely that students will want to continue learning, past formal experiences, if their true "reward" for learning (working) has been merely to have the gruesome experience stop. The secret for developing capacity for work is to stretch the length of time between *rewards* so that the student will strive through some misery to seek long-term goals, e.g., a college degree, continued reading of great literature, ongoing enjoyment in listening to music masterworks, or an insatiable desire for scientific precision.

Thus, the problem for the teacher is not only to make work tasks pleasurable but also to develop capacity for work. *This constitutes a process of teaching for delayed rewards over an ever-increasing temporal span.* **What if it's work?—Then work it must be and the capacity for work must be developed.**

3

LEARNING

The Modification of Behavior

What is behavior modification?

Behavior is a common word which is used quite casually in reference to many things. Behavior is used in this book to refer to *anything* a person does, says, or thinks that can be observed directly and/or indirectly. Besides referring to specific stimulus-response effects, behavior modification includes techniques of changing behavior. A well-behaved child is a child that behaves in ways the teacher thinks are appropriate to the situation.

Some people try to make a case against a behavioral approach by alluding to many "attitudes" that are not a part of the processes of behavior modification. Rather, these "attitudes" represent different value systems. *Principles* for teaching (shaping) appropriate behaviors should not be confused with other issues. Many teachers regard the questions of why, what, and who as certainly more important than how. Therefore, after the teacher has decided what is to be learned, why it should be learned, and who is going to learn it, then a behavioral approach will help the teacher go about teaching it. There is a very simple rationale to explain the efficacy of behavioral approaches. Simply stated, *behavioral change must be based on a reason:* children work for things that bring them pleasure, children work for approval of people they love, children change behaviors to satisfy the desires they have been taught to value, children avoid behaviors they associate with unpleasantness, and children act in similar ways to behaviors they have often repeated. The behavior modification approach actually comes from science, and represents nothing more than simple cause-and-effect relationships.

Some teachers might say, "Yes, but isn't that a cold approach?" Certainly not. While behavior modification is based on scientific principles verified in the laboratory, it is largely the nature of material to be learned that represents important value choices. (Incidentally, *who* decides children should learn to read? Whose values?) Actually, because of its consistency and simplicity, behavioral modification effected through contingent reinforcement (approval-disapproval) represents a very kind and understandable system to children. The behavioral scientist who observes a classroom can behaviorally classify almost everything that goes on, regardless of how well the teacher may understand principles of reinforcement. Cause-and-effect behaviors are always present. For example, some teachers do not realize when they are being sarcastic.) "Why don't you just stand up and tell the *whole class,* Jimmy?" Thus, problems are created because the student is not really sure of the teacher's meaning. Being taken literally is the price one pays for using sarcasm. Even adults are often not sure in deciding what is sarcastic. The scientist could demonstrate how the teacher might be more effective in the application of the teacher's values. Many teachers are surprised to learn how closely they approximate a strict behavioral approach. After being apprised of behavioral principles many teachers exclaim, "Why, that's what I've been doing all the time!"

When learning is defined as a change or modification of behavior, then three things are necessary: (1) experience, (2) discrimination, and (3) association. For instance, a child is presented with a color *(experience).* After a time the child *discriminates* the color from other colors or the absence of the color. Through repetition, an *association(s)* is made with the color, e.g., red. The child may then evidence in some behavior, most often previously learned, (e.g., pointing, matching, speaking, thinking) that he has learned the color. The preceding definition of learning based upon reinforcement theory does not quarrel with mediational processes in learning or with the material to be learned. It proposes a method to promote or expedite this learning. In short, it asks, "How should we go about teaching the color red in the best possible manner to insure correct association?" If the child responds favorably to teaching, we assume the external stimuli are associated in a way which functions as a reward for the child. But what if the child does not respond? Then we must restructure the external environment whereby the child does receive proper motivation. **What is behavior modification?—It is a process for learning.**

Is subject matter discipline?

(The recent impetus for behavioral theory, or reinforcement theory, or whatever one chooses to call behavioral principles, substantially grew from the works of B. F. Skinner. Programmed instruction is the best-known result of this initial work, as are many other "systems" relating to teaching, treating mental illness, behavioral research, and clinical psychology.) Indeed, the entire rationale concerning behavior modification is that behavior is *learned.* What behavior? *All behavior, including knowledge of subject matter.* Behavior thusly defined includes emotional responses, attitudes, reading, listening, talking, looking into the mirror, liking a person, wanting to talk out a problem, hitting, being frustrated, staying on task, getting off task, responding appropriately to the desires of a teacher, not responding to the desires of a teacher, all 'good" behavior, all "bad" behavior, disturbing the class, being well behaved, being excited about learning, hating to learn, and so on—and so on—and so on.

(The most basic reductions of reinforcement theory as an explanation to assess a person's responses at any given time are: (1) a person has *not learned,* (2) he has learned correct associations, or (3) he has learned *incorrect associations.* Exactly the same principles are used to teach subject matter as are used to teach appropriate social skills. If the teacher wishes that children have a real desire to learn a particular subject matter, the teacher must structure the external environment so that children will seek the structured contingent rewards for their academic work tasks.) After initial manipulation the rewards for learning will often come from the reinforcement of the learning material itself. Incidentally, this is precisely what most teachers do when they initially make a "game out of learning." The children become enthused concerning the game *per se,* not realizing it is a subtle hoax to stimulate effective learning. Curiously, some teachers who try desperately to make learning "fun" also say they reject any "manipulation techniques." The teacher's job is to structure learning experiences. This structuring process involves manipulating the environment conducive to effective learning, whether the goal be simple word associations, complex problem solving, or concept formation. It would seem that the teacher should structure as wisely as possible. One should know the subparts necessary to any complex academic task (e.g., English, reading, algebra, history) and structure the situation in order that each child have a "rewarding learning experience." It can be seen that even in reference to our most cherished clichés, we actually do practice behavioral manipulation. It appears paradoxical for the teacher to reject manipulation when this is indeed the essence of the teacher's work.

Behavioral research demonstrates that if subject matter can be: (1) geared to the student at his own level, (2) presented in logical sequences, with (3) appropriate feedback concerning correct/incorrect responses, and (4) contingent rewards given for successive approximations toward defined goals, then *learning will certainly take place.* Exactly the same principles apply to teaching subject matter as apply to teaching social skills. **Is subject matter discipline?—Yes.**

Are goals necessary?

Traditionally, teachers have been instructed to prepare goals for the classroom. This usually represents at best a vague effort, often after the fact, to state formally what the learning experiences are aimed toward, i.e., what should be the learning outcome. The major problem regarding goals is that they are usually stated in euphonious clichés: "preparation for life in a democracy," "to develop language skills," "to understand the different cultures of the world," "to develop an appreciation for music." What do such statements tell us? How will we know if we have achieved our "goals"? Some educators try to solve the problem by proposing even greater hierarchies, including ideals, objectives, attitudes, and so on. The problem is easily solved, however, if the teacher states goals that represent overt behavioral changes. How else, incidentally, will we know that a student "understands" or has "learned"? The teacher must also decide whose goals are to be effected in the classroom: students', parents', administrators', and/or what combination.

Goals stated in behavioral terms are not only manageable, they are also clear in defining the behaviors to be learned: "to be able to verbalize the Constitution, giving dictionary definitions to all words found therein," "to recognize on a map the separate nations of the world," to differentiate between ten musical compositions," "to have a reading, writing, and spelling vocabulary of three hundred selected words." If concepts such as appreciation, understanding, or attitudes are to have meaning, these meanings should be defined in ways conducive to assessment. It is very easy to hide behind such generalities. *If children are to learn, then we must know precisely what it is they are to learn, how to teach it to them, and also how to determine if they have learned it.* **Are goals necessary?–Certainly.**

Can behavior be measured?

Formal and informal tests have always provided indications of academic behavioral change. Other indices of measurement, especially relating to social skills, have previously seemed to defy classification. However, it *is* possible for the teacher to learn classifying scales to assess *social* behaviors. The only difficulty regarding these classification procedures is that they take a little extra effort. *Behavior occurs in time intervals.* If the teacher is to know whether a particular behavior is getting worse, better, or staying the same, the frequency of behavioral occurrences must be recorded in time intervals. Recording procedures are not difficult; one needs only paper, pencil, and some measure of time (clock).

For example, what if undesirable behavior in a particular class-room is defined as "standing up"? Instead of doing work at their desks, many students walk around the room. The first procedure would be to know precisely how much standing up is taking place (base line). If this recording does not take place and the teacher first takes remedial steps, then it will not be known if the undesired behavior is getting better, worse, or staying the same. It may seem that this procedure is not necessary. "Why not just tell them to sit down and see what happens?" The problem, however, arises *in time;* i.e., some children will sit down immediately, but in the *long run,* more children may stand. Even if the standing students do sit immediately, the problem is not solved; it continues with the other students in time. To conduct this type of recording, the teacher might assign a work task and then sit so as to see every student and count the number of children standing in a number of ten-second intervals. After a few days of recording the number of such behavioral occurrences on one individual or on many, the teacher has some idea of the *frequency of the behavior*. A checklist at the students' desks can also be very effective.

The same basic procedure may be used for speaking out, talking, playing at desk, looking out the window, cheating, hitting, sharpening pencils, disturbing others, crying, or any other conceivable behavior (adaptive or deviant). It is important for the teacher to have a record for *social behaviors* as well as for academic behaviors. A general "all right" or "satisfactory" will not accurately assess a student's academic progress over a period of time; neither will it accurately assess his social behavior. The time these behaviors take to record does not compare to the time a teacher spends repeating instructions (nagging). It is interesting that one of the author's experimental teachers who absolutely refused to "waste my time with all that book work" was recorded by experimental observers saying, "Now stop that talking," 143 times in one morning session. Checklists for assignments of any kind may be developed (see pages 43-111). This process represents nothing more than extending principles of record keeping, but *in time intervals*. **Can behavior be measured?—Easily.**

4

BEHAVIOR

The Contingent Result of Life

The reader has been exposed to some basic questions regarding discipline. This chapter offers instruction in *how to discipline*. It is devoted to inappropriate behavior, although the same principles apply to appropriate responses (wholesome learning).

What is the payoff?

A traditional viewpoint prevalent in education is to focus upon many antecedent events (reinforcement history) leading toward a particular behavioral goal, rather than to focus upon the manipulation and control of the present environment. This procedure of looking backward is both unproductive and unnecessary, especially when it absolves the responsibility of solving the current problem. When the teacher wants to change a specific inappropriate behavior, the teacher must first *find the payoff* and eliminate it if possible. **Behavior that goes unrewarded will extinguish.** The teacher must watch the student carefully to determine the payoff. The teacher must also recognize individual differences; the payoff is often different for each child. For example, students A, B, and C talk in class. After many warnings the teacher finally sends them to the principal's office. This is just exactly what student A wanted; he finally managed to goad the teacher into "punishing" him. Student B just liked to make the teacher angry. Every time she got stern it just "broke him up." He knew he was bothering her, and he enjoyed her distress—"Wow! She gave me such *stern* looks." Student C did not care about the teacher or the principal. He did care about students A and B. Every time he talked, they listened. On the way to the principal's office, student A filled the others in. "Listen, the principal sits you down and comes on with all this 'You've got to be a good boy' stuff. Man, the last time I was in there I really had him snowed. Besides, he never checks to see if you go back to the class, so we're out for the day." When students A, B, and C return to class, they will continue to talk—even more.

Teachers who have simple monolithic explanations for all maladaptive behaviors will be generally ineffective. "All those children need is a little love." "The thing they need is a good hard paddling." "Get them out in the world; then you'll see how they do." "They need a decent place to live." "They need someone who truly understands them." The problem with this type of analysis is that it is not differentiated. There are some children who may fit one, none, or all of the above categories, plus countless others. The one thing that children exhibiting inappropriate responses *do* need is a teacher who can find the payoff. What is keeping the behavior alive? If the payoff can be found and completely eliminated, then the behavior will gradually extinguish—*if consistency is maintained.*

One significant result of eliminating the payoff is that the undesired behavior will get initially worse before it gets better. The teacher must remember that the student has learned a behavior to get what he wants. When the "reward" is abolished, he tries even harder (i.e., the inappropriate behavior increases) before he comes to realize that there is no payoff. After this initial surge the behavior will extinguish. This initial rise is extremely important to remember. Many people give up during the storm before the calm. "Oh, I've tried ignoring, but the baby cried even louder." —Of course.

Finding the payoff can be difficult, and sometimes the payoff comes from a source that the teacher cannot control (parents, peers etc.). Nevertheless, many problems can be solved by cutting out the "reward." **What is the payoff?—That which keeps the behavior alive.**
P.S. Give student A a task much less desirable than talking in class, preferably where he can't talk to anyone—isolation. Smile at student B when he is not talking; absolutely ignore him when he is. Move student

C to the other side of the room away from students A and B, or make him apologize in front of the room, or perhaps even punish students A and B and tell them it's not their fault but student C's.

What constitutes reward?

After the teacher determines the payoff and eliminates it, the teacher will soon observe a decrease in undesirable behavior. Sometimes this alone is all that is needed. Yet more often the teacher must control other stimuli (i.e., structure contingencies) in order to discipline. It is better to start with just one behavior and not try to eliminate everything simultaneously, unless the teacher has a great deal of help and can initially devote all the time just to social behavioral problems. If many maladaptive behaviors are prevalent throughout the classroom, the teacher is advised to establish a hierarchy and start with the deviant behavior that most interferes with learning. It is also advisable to make up a set of easily understood rules for the classroom. In making up the contingencies (i.e., structuring the rewards) the new payoff for *desirable* behavior (following the rules) must be known, tangible, and close enough to the student's own behavioral responses to motivate the student to seek it. Initially it is better to give too much reward than not enough. The idea is to get the students winning as soon as possible. For general classroom control in the elementary grades, various "token systems" are highly effective; group activities and peer group approval are also effective for the junior high and high school years. Token systems come closest to representing our social monetary system. Correct responses earn "tokens" that are exchanged for tangible goods (e.g., toys or classroom materials which do not need to be expensive). Rewards earned for tokens should have marked values (i.e., colored paper — 30 points, ruler — 50 points, glider plane — 80 points) so that students can receive tangible credit for following the rules (written on the board and explained daily). Each child can have a small notebook on the upper left corner of his desk, and at appropriate intervals the teacher marks the student's points. The teacher may start the morning by holding up the rewards and asking the children which one they are working toward. Then the teacher may go over the rules: We sit quietly during individual study. We raise our hand before we talk. We stay at our own desk unless given permission by the teacher, etc. At opportune times the teacher circulates, writing down the points. The very act of recording may be used as an effective control. Sometimes the teacher will want to *catch a child being good* and reward him with points instantaneously.

In the initial stages of control it is important to have the child achieve success quickly, after which the time between behavior and reward may be stretched for longer periods while pairing with appropriate personal responses from the teacher (praising, smiling, touching). In time the personal approval of the teacher or even self-approval will probably be all that is needed for proper motivation. This is certainly what every teacher desires, but in order to achieve this level of sophistication, one must start where the child is. Some children enter school with response expectations amenable to smiling, pleasing the teacher, being obedient, etc. Others have to learn appropriate responses through more tangible rewards.

One extremely effective technique for small children is the use of food (M & M's, juice, flavored cereal). The teacher may start the very first class with an M & M party. While the children are eating, the teacher says, "We will have another M & M party if everyone is quiet while I count to ten." (The teacher counts aloud quickly, making sure they win.) After giving the candy the teacher says, "If everyone is quiet for five minutes we will have another party, but if someone talks we will not get to have one." Now the teacher sits back and waits; in all probability someone will talk, whereupon the teacher says, "Oh, I'm *very sorry*. Mary talked before our time was up; now we will not get to have a party. Maybe tomorrow we may have one if everyone is quiet." (Some children will think this is not "fair.") *Because the teacher does not get angry at Mary, Mary cannot give her problem to the teacher.* Mary receives the disapproval of the group so there is no payoff from the other children. Instead of interacting directly with Mary, it may be better to use vicarious reinforcement and modeling. To use this technique the teacher chooses one of the most well-behaved children and says, "I surely like the way Sheila is sitting so quietly. If everyone behaved like Sheila, we could have our party." Sometimes the teacher may wish to give rewards to those children who were quiet and not give anything to those who were not. (Mary may not think this is fair.)

The use of group approval-disapproval is very effective, particularly with older students. When activities are given or denied, contingent upon the behavior of all students, the students themselves will take the responsibility for discipline; and discipline will start to evolve from within the group. *Peer approval* is extremely important to older students. This is precisely the reason for such high *esprit de corps* in many student organizations, such as band, athletics, social clubs, gangs, etc. When teacher and students are taught to cut out the payoff for an individual's deviant responses, the student's maladaptive behavior extinguishes. Some students are indeed embarrassed after receiving such responses from the teacher or their peers—so be it.

Rewards the teacher can use contingently include: (1) words (spoken and written—rules), (2) expressions (facial—bodily), (3) closeness (nearness—touching), (4) activities and privileges (social—individual), and (5) things (materials—food—playthings—awards). Other than subject matter itself, these categories constitute the *entire resources* the teacher has for structuring. The teacher should develop them well. (See lists on pages 116-131.) **What constitutes reward?—That which the student will work toward.**

Is the world fair?

For years teachers have been advocating the uniqueness of every student. "All children are not alike," they say. "Each child has had many different experiences"; "children come from many different backgrounds"; "they need individual attention." One would assume from this dedication to individual difference that teachers would teach differentially and meet the discipline problems of each child in a unique manner, but this does not seem to be the case. Most teachers also seem preoccupied with an undifferentiated concept of "fairness."

Children do not have a problem with undifferentiated "fairness" until someone teaches it to them. Usually it is taught by their parents, who manifest the same thinking as some teachers. With little hesitation, parents will talk at length about how different their children are. Equally without hesitation, they try as hard as possible to be "fair." Fred and Jane are different in many, many ways. They like different things, they respond differently, and one child is almost always older. Yet, when Fred gets to go, Jane gets to go; when Jane gets candy, Fred must have candy. If Fred receives a toy, Jane must, also. Fred and Jane learn quickly "Why can't I stay up late?"; "Why don't I get to go?"; "How come I don't get a present?"; "Why does she always get the biggest apple?" Thus Mother and Dad spend a great deal of time and energy trying to be "fair." They also create much anxiety for themselves by not admitting that they do treat the children differently and from time to time may actually even like one child more than another. These are all unnecessary attempts designed to solve the problem of undifferentiated fairness they have created for themselves. "But Fred, your birthday will come next month," "Jane, you see Fred is older than you; that's why he stays up later." "OK, if you're going to fight over who gets the biggest apple, neither one of you can have one."

People *are* different. Some are extremely different, particularly if they have physical or mental handicaps. It would seem that the kindest teaching behavior would be to instruct children in this regard—let them know that the world is not always "fair." Prepare them for the suffering they will endure because of others' mistakes. Let them realize from the beginning that their efforts are not always evaluated fairly. Help them understand that in a democracy the group often suffers from the actions of a few. Let them realize that occasionally they will be punished for things that they do not do. Teach them to understand that justice is an ideal, less often a reality. *Yes, and also instruct them to be just in their own personal behaviors, but not always to expect it from others.* Some of the gravest problems encountered by children come from an undifferentiated concept of "fairness."

Fairness is not a simple matter. Men have labored for centuries to ascertain "what's fair" in relationship to many different situations (laws). Within the academic realm, the teacher also works hard at differential assessment. Grades are assigned differentially as are special projects, reports, reading groups, and so on. Thus, *the teacher* establishes rules of academic discriminations (fairness?). How naïve, then, to equip the child with one social response the teacher knows will cause him problems as he matures. The teacher also loses a most effective technique (group approval—disapproval) when refusing to use the group in "shaping up" individuals, for to punish the group because of one individual or vice versa does not seem "fair." Ideally, proper interaction patterns will eventually evolve from within the group. Children will help discipline each other, not by punishing, but by ignoring, attending to what is proper, not talking or listening to each other when they should not be, and generally *staying on task.* However, discipline will not evolve from the group unless the teacher uses the group to bring particular individuals "in line."

No one wishes to be punished for another's actions. However, in cooperative societies this goes on continuously. If elected officials in a representative government decide to enter a war, they do not ask the individual student. If a student in the bud of maturity is drafted, fights, and subsequently dies in battle, then who suffers? Why not prepare a child for the world in which he lives, where everyone's life is affected by the acts of others? Let him realize early that if he is to function socially he must take the responsibility and the results of interacting with others—he does not stand alone. Help students understand that "what's fair" is a very big question relating differentially to almost all aspects of life. Do not prepare them for certain disillusionment with one undifferentiated response. Help them discriminate between the many issues of fairness and be prepared to deal realistically with these discernments. Students may then come to accept life's inequities while doing something to change many of them, rather than feeling sorry for themselves because they find some aspects of interaction "unfair." When the teacher deals with fairness, optimism need not suffer—only naïveté. **Is the world fair?—Sometimes.**

Can contingencies be structured?

The basic premise of reinforcement teaching is to arrange the stimuli of the external world to shape the behavior of the students—to structure the environment so that the student receives approval-disapproval reinforcements contingent upon appropriate/inappropriate behavior. Therefore, *reinforcement teaching is the structure of approval and disapproval reinforcers, in time, to shape desired behavior toward specific goals.* Experimentation in learning demonstrates that: (a) If a student knows specifically what is expected of him, and (b) he wants to do it, then (c) he probably will. The necessity for specific measurable goals (expectations for students) has already been mentioned. The crux of the problem rests with (b): arranging the contingencies of reinforcement so that a student will want to do what the teacher expects.

Five techniques used in structuring contingencies are:

1. *Approval* (rewards)
2. *Withholding of approval—withholding rewards* (hope)
3. *Disapproval* (punishment)

4. *Threat of disapproval* (fear)

5. *Ignoring* (not attending in any manner)

1. Approval is easily understood. Approval is anything that is generally related with *happiness,* such as food, candy, smiling, touching, attention, praise, proximity, clothes, cars, etc. The teacher must be sure, however, that what the teacher believes is functioning as a positive reinforcer is truly positive (some children don't like ice cream).

2. Withholding of approval (withholding rewards) is used when the positive reinforcer has previously been established. Withholding the positive reinforcer probably functions to produce "hope for the attainment of a reward the next time—if the behavior is improved." In a way this procedure acts as "punishment," although with greater effect and less wear and tear on everyone concerned. "I'm so sorry you didn't finish on time. Now we cannot go out to play. Perhaps tomorrow you will finish on time. Then you may play."

3. Disapproval is also easily understood. Disapproval is generally synonymous with *unhappiness,* such as frowning, getting yelled at, being frightened, put in isolation, embarrassed, being made to do an unpleasant task, etc. The teacher must also be careful here not to ascribe monolithic judgment concerning what constitutes disapproval. Maladaptive children often exhibit many perverted associations. "I like to get spanked." "I enjoy making the teacher angry." Extreme disapproval (corporal punishment) should be used very sparingly, if at all.

4. Threat of disapproval (fear). This also should be rare; yet it is profoundly effective once the knowledge of disapproval is established. This procedure leads to a way of behaving to avoid disapproval (unpleasant stimuli): "I am careful when crossing the road to avoid getting killed"; "I don't play with guns because I could get shot"; "I study so I won't fail"; "I act appropriately in class so as to avoid the disapproval of the teacher," etc. While fear is an extremely effective suppressant, it does little in establishing the joy of learning. Children who are completely negatively motivated usually are tense, unenthusiastic, quiet, shy, passive, and generally fearful. Some of these children do eventually succeed, although this negatively motivated "success" usually comes at the high price of guilt, compulsiveness, generalized anxiety, and, perhaps later, even ulcers.

5. Ignore—just that—ignore.

The following formula represents a simple interaction for behavioral shaping:

STUDENT BEHAVIOR

	Appropriate Social and Academic	*Inappropriate* Social and Academic
Approval	Yes	No
Witholding of Approval	No	Yes
Disapproval	No	Yes (unless "payoff")
Threat of Disapproval	No	Yes
Ignore	No	Yes (unless dangerous)

TEACHER BEHAVIOR

The teacher is advised, if at all possible, to use primarily approval, withholding of approval, and ignoring in controlling behavior. There is some indication that these "positive approaches" may be more effective, but more important, *much less damage can be done than through the use of punishments.* This does *not* mean the teacher should be permissive. It indicates that as the teacher structures the child's environment contingent on appropriate behaviors, the teacher should diligently try to do so through the use of "positive" techniques and structuring incompatible responses. Alternately, there are times when punishment might need to be used. Some maladaptive behaviors of children are much worse than the punishment it could take to eliminate them. **Can contingencies be structured?—They must!**

5

LIFE

The Structure of Activities in Time

Is time important?

Thank you, reader. Thank you for what? Thank you for reading the next paragraph. You have not read it yet? Oh.

Why is the preceding rather absurd? It is because the "thank you" comes before the fact. Therefore, it has little meaning and even less significance in modifying your behavior (except perhaps in creating confusion). In all the experimental laboratory research concerned with behavior, no one has ever been able to teach anything through the use of antecedent rewards. *Rewards must come after the fact.* Thus, we enter the most elusive aspect of teaching—time. All events take place in time. B. Franklin has this maxim: "Dost thou love life? Then do not squander time, for that is the stuff life is made of."

One of the most basic differentiations of the growing child comes in his progressive sophistication regarding time. Even adults cannot really tell time, as evidenced by the chronoscopes we strap to our arms. Man's temporal span is exceedingly short, and our assessment of ongoing time becomes humorous (try to estimate a minute without counting to yourself)! Even with a minute you must "fill it up with something" in order to approximate the passage of time. Now consider these foolish temporal contingencies: One-year-old: "Baby knows I'll pick her up after I finish my work." Three-year-old: "Tomorrow we will go out to play." Six-year-old: "Next week is party time." Nine-year-old: "When you get to be eleven, you may join the scouts." Thirteen-year-old: "If you pass all your classes, you may have a car when you're sixteen." Sixteen-year-old: "You must graduate from college if you expect to have a good life." College freshman: "Study diligently and you will be a good teacher." If these sequences sound long, try a few out on yourself just to see how close a contingent reward or punishment must be in time to motivate you. "One more drink and tomorrow morning, wow!" "You don't have the money—why not just charge it?" "Better stop this late discussion—8:00 A.M. comes early," or "Better start studying—final exams in just two weeks." As you can see, your temporal motivation is *not* long at all. Of course you realize the necessity of working toward or avoiding all those things, but they are up there in time somewhere—not now—not close enough in time to really motivate *you.*

If contingent rewards/punishments for behavior are to be effective, they must take place immediately, and *the teacher must always know, before the fact, just what the contingencies are to be.* With small children this is tremendously important. "Daddy's going to spank you when he gets home" is a typical example of a ridiculous contingency.

It is also important to correct any deviant behavior before it becomes full-blown—to nip it in the bud. The teacher who believes that a small disturbance "will get better" is right. It will get better and better and *better* and **better!** Full-blown disorder is usually encouraged by hesitation and caused by self-deception. *Initial stages of control are the most important.* As the child matures, his temporal span will increase *if* he is taught proper behaviors while progressively lengthening the time between action and consequence. If the bag of oats is too close to the horse, he eats the oats; if the bag is too far away, he does not move. **Time and the control of reinforcement schedules in time is imperative.** Reinforcers can be delivered on many different schedules depending on the circumstances (fixed time, fixed interval, variable time, variable interval, or mixed). The job of the teacher is to meet the student where he is and then progressively take him to the point where he will be content to wait for longer and longer rewards while still exhibiting proper behavior (e.g., structuring progressive work tasks toward final grades). Actually, many people guard time more jealously than anything over which they have control. *The art of living evolves from the structure of meaningful activities in time.* **Is time important?—Time is life.**

Is consistency difficult?

If one were to take the principle *"Behavior that is partially reinforced is the most difficult to extinguish"* and asked to devise a system whereby he could make a million dollars through its use, one might come up with gambling. Gambling is an activity that represents partial reinforcement at its best. If a gambler knows he will always lose, he will not gamble. Obviously he cannot always win, so the trick is to structure the environment (e.g., set the odds in a machine or roulette wheel) so that he *wins* often enough to *lose* his money in the long run .

Such is the case with other behavior. The child does not remember the 1,321 times he went to bed at 8:00 P.M. He remembers the two times he got to stay up. The third grader does not really believe that the teacher will send him to "the time-out room (isolation) for ten minutes." This is already the sixth time the teacher has threatened and nothing has happened yet. The ninth grader cheated before and didn't get caught; why should he get caught this time? The college student has turned in late papers before; why should this professor be such a "hard nose"?

Inconsistency teaches just that—inconsistency. At best it produces gambling children, at worst large-scale mental illness. *The most difficult task for a teacher is consistency!* The teacher should think about how the contingencies are to be structured, make the rules, and *follow through.* The only thing that you teach a child when you break the rules is just that—to break the rules. How pathetic it is to observe children who have many severe maladaptive behaviors that have been allowed to fester for longer and longer periods because of partial reinforcement. It is much like *favorable* responses; we stretch the temporal spans between reinforcement to provide longer periods of productive activity. In maladaptive responses some children's reinforcement history contains so much partial reinforcement they will fight for weeks and months before giving up their learned behaviors. **Is consistency difficult?—It is the most difficult aspect of discipline.**

If at first you don't succeed?

If behaviors can be learned, they can also be unlearned or

relearned. Sometimes in our zeal to get through to our students, we make mistakes. Sometimes regardless of zeal, we make mistakes. The efficacy of behavioral techniques with *severe* problem behaviors within mental hospitals and institutions for the retarded and handicapped should give us the courage to move forward. Behavioral techniques have demonstrated that even severely handicapped children can learn much faster and a great deal more than we previously believed possible.

Since it is impossible for the student to maintain two contradictory responses at the same time, the skillful teacher will program to elicit responses *incompatible* with deviant behavior. "Count to ten before you get angry; think before you begin your work; raise your hand before you talk; take three big breaths before you cry; speak softly so we can have a 'soft' argument; now we are practicing *good* grammar; let's take a break so we can begin with freshness; I'll close the curtain so the outside will not distract us; let's put our other materials away before we begin the new activity," and so on. Punishment alone may stop deviant behavior, but it will not necessarily teach correct associations. The child who is hit with his spoon because he cannot use it properly will not necessarily learn proper etiquette. Similarly, the student who is punished for his bad writing will not necessarily learn to write correctly. The one child might shun the spoon; the other student may stop writing. Teaching for incompatible responses is perhaps the most effective behavioral technique because it constitutes a double-edged approach. Not only is the inappropriate behavior eliminated, but it is replaced by a correct response as well. Thus the student unlearns and relearns at the same time. It should be obvious that in this case appropriate responses are directly proportional to decreases in inappropriate responses. This procedure eliminates the need for punishment and at the same time teaches correct associations. However, the teacher must deal with *overt* behaviors. *It is much easier to act your way into a new way of thinking than to think your way into a new way of acting.*

Four principles* for the teacher are:

1. *Pinpoint:* It is necessary to pinpoint explicitly the behavior that is to be eliminated or established. This takes place at many different

*These principles were adapted from the work of O. R. Lindsley, "Teaching Teachers to Teach," a paper presented at the American Psychological Association Convention, New York, September, 1966.

levels relating to many differentiated behaviors. It leads to a hierarchical arrangement of skills and behaviors based upon expected specific behavioral goals. Do not deal with intangibles. If the behavior cannot in some way be measured, then you can never know if it has been learned or unlearned.

2. *Record:* List the specified behaviors in time, and thereby establish a precise record from which to proceed. Keep the record accurate. Do not guess; be scientific. As maladaptive responses are eliminated, more time can be devoted to more productive learning.

3. *Consequate:* Set up the external environmental contingencies (including primarily your own personal responses) and proceed with the program. Contingencies include approval, withdrawal of approval, disapproval, threat of disapproval, or ignoring. Reinforcers may be words (spoken—written), expressions (facial—bodily), closeness (nearness—touching), activities (social—individual), and things (materials—food—playthings—awards). Remember that when you ignore, behaviors often initially increase (sometimes for long periods) before they are eliminated.

4. *Evaluate:* Be prepared to stay with a program long enough to ascertain its effectiveness. Learn from your mistakes. And **"If at first you don't succeed"**—well, you know.

Teaching—art or science?

The question will continue to be asked, "What makes a good teacher?" We have all known some truly great teachers as well as others who wane by comparison. Analyzing teaching behavior is really no different from analyzing student behavior. Earlier it was stated that students must know what is expected of them and want to do it. Most teachers have at least a general idea of what is expected of them and also want to be good teachers. However, if they do not practice techniques of effective classroom control and subject-matter presentation, they fail. Every principle relating to student behavior throughout the preceding chapters also applies to the teacher. However, it is much more important that the teacher realize *it is the teacher's responsibility* to insure that learning actually takes place—not the student's. How easy it is for some teachers to give *their* problem to the students. "They don't want to learn." "I can't wait to get out of this blackboard jungle." "Why should I care if the students don't?" Perhaps the extreme of this attitude is manifest by some college teachers who judge their academic prowess by how many students they fail. The teacher who really cares will persevere. Through trial and error the teacher will find better ways to stimulate students toward their optimum potentials. With or without a full understanding of behavioral principles, the teacher will come to find better methods of behavioral control and subject-matter presentation.

The ability to recognize individual differences and to structure a class environment with meaningful contingencies relevant to specific situations represents an outstanding accomplishment. However, good taste is also of major importance. The authors know of one seventh-grade teacher who controlled her class by having the most deviant children "participate in a mock wedding ceremony if they were very, very bad." When the children evidenced proper behaviors, they were then allowed to "get divorced." This disciplinary procedure was tremendously effective and used behavioral principles. However, it raises serious questions regarding the teaching of other associations. Another teacher told of a technique she used with second-grade boys. "When a boy misbehaves, I make him wear a girl's ribbon in his hair." Does it work? Very well, but again we question the advisability of such insensitivity toward teaching. proper sex identification. It is ironic that this same teacher thought it "terrible" that parents were asked to send their children to school without breakfast occasionally in order to effect proper behaviors through *rewards* of cookies, cereal, and milk.

It is readily apparent that regardless of how many "behavioral recipes" are available, the insensitive teacher will still be found wanting. The art of teaching seems directly contingent upon the behaviors of the teacher as a person. Modeling effects assimilated through the influence of an outstanding individual are still some of the most powerful and far-reaching. Most teachers will allude to a special teacher in their past who influenced them tremendously, even to the point of going into the profession. The truly effective teacher will combine the science of behavior with the art of living to create that exceptionally rare atmosphere—an environment where children not only take excitement from discovery but learn to be nice people.

PART II

Behavioral Principles Applied

6

CHANGING WRONG ASSOCIATIONS

The preceding essays comprising Part I were not presented to express maverick points of view. These issues were developed to prepare the teacher to deal with human behavior more objectively. It is extremely easy to make-believe, to pretend that behavior is mystical and that somehow children will learn the opposite of what they are taught. Are the fine, gifted students direct products of our inspired teaching, while the slow, mischievous or dull students products of someone else? If we are honest, we must take our share of the grief as well as the joy. Perhaps the most frightening aspect of teaching is that behavior is most certainly learned, and, for this, we as teachers must take full responsibility. Pretending is easier, for discipline is an awesome challenge. We prefer to believe that the deviant child will somehow change—that his bad behavior is just a stage, or if only he could work it out of his system everything would be all right. We hope, but hope wears thin without positive signs of improvement. We struggle, we wait, we often become discouraged, and finally we realize that it is indeed a cause-and-effect world—in the long run we do "reap that which we sow." After myths are laid aside; after the teacher stops worrying and starts acting; after personal beliefs, consistency, and individual responsibility are all in harmony—the teacher begins to teach. Subsequently, behavior becomes more predictable and effects of specific actions assured. As behavioral principles are practiced and applied, the teacher becomes confident that *wrong associations can indeed be changed.*

The following examples represent selected scientific and professional applications of behavioral changing. These excerpts are presented in a form that should be easily understood by teachers. *Scientific Applications* are summaries of scientific studies that have been published in journals or presented by researchers at scientific conventions. Sources for these reports are listed numerically and presented on pages 138-39. *Professional Applications* represent the attempts of "ordinary" teachers to deal with classroom problems systematically. These examples are selected from the authors' files.

This cryptic format does not begin to do justice to the original reports. The thoughtful reader will not only seek other professional examples directly applicable to his own teaching situation but will also begin to read original scientific literature and to study carefully the cause-and-effect relationships obviously evidenced in behavioral research. It is important for the teacher to understand the principles underlying discipline before choosing specific techniques. Processes and principles are of much greater consequence than the choice of reinforcers. When processes of education are fully understood, fanciful gimmicks become sound pedagogy.

Pinpoint: *Bothering teacher at desk.*
                       (4th grade)

Record: Students unnecessarily at teacher's desk
                       (twenty-eight occurrences—one week).

Consequate: Teacher *ignored* all children who came to
                       desk—made no eye contact, said nothing.
                       Teacher recognized only those children who
                       raised hands at seats.

Evaluate: Occurrences of students at teacher's desk
                       steadily decreased. After two weeks, daily
                       average between zero and one.

Professional Application

Pinpoint: *Teasing other children.*
                       (Individual student, 4th grade)

Record: Disruptive behavior 83% (teacher's obser-
                       vation—two days).

Consequate: *Isolation.* A coatrack and bookcase rearranged
                       in back of classroom, making small isolation
                       cubicle for child. Child sent to this "time-out
                       place" for ten minutes every time he dis-
                       rupted class.

Evaluate: Disruptive behavior steadily *decreased.* After
                       nine isolations (four during first day) disrup-
                       tive behavior dropped to 10%.
                       Note: This child's teasing behavior was
                       probably producing "payoff" from class
                       (laughing, complaining, attending).

Professional Application

Pinpoint: *Inappropriate pencil sharpening.*
(3rd grade)

Record: Substitute teacher noticed two children going to pencil sharpener, then five, then entire class.

Consequate: Substitute got up from desk, gently removed sharpener bin, told children she would read a story if they completed work during next twenty minutes. They did—she did.

Evaluate: A pleasant day.
Note: Any teacher, especially a substitute, must catch a problem immediately.

Professional Application

Pinpoint:	*Overactivity.*
	(Six boys, 9 to 13 years, low-level intelligence)
Record:	Boys observed in playroom for eight days.
Consequate:	Rewarded following thirty seconds of "quiet time" (tokens exchangeable for candy). Procedure continued thirty days; during last four days token given after forty-five seconds.
Evaluate:	Overactivity reduced 67%.
	Note: Overactivity was still substantially decreased eight days later when *no rewards* were used.

Scientific Application[1]

Pinpoint: *Littering.*
(6th grade)

Record: Materials not put away—twenty-five daily (average one week).

Consequate: Large FRIDAY BOX instituted in classroom. Each student given responsibility for own materials—individually labeled. Materials not put away went in Friday Box. Friday Box opened one half-hour weekly—*only then could articles be recovered.*

Evaluate: After second week of Friday Box, littering decreased to three incidents weekly.
Note: This procedure seems effective in all situations and at all age levels. An author had to wait four days to recover important research materials placed by his wife in the family Sunday Box. Also, the amount of material not taken from the box that is allowed to remain week after week provides a good indication of its worth to the litterer.

Professional Application

Pinpoint: *Early arithmetic reasoning.*
                             (one male, 3.5; one female, 3)

Record: Completed arithmetic assignments zero.

Consequate: Students learned numbers through pushing
                             buttons which turned lights on and off. No ver-
                             bal communication used. Tasks ordered and re-
                             duced to very small steps. Correct responses
                             immediately followed by a tone. Food re-
                             wards given on preset schedule for correct
                             responses. Incorrect responses resulted in short
                             blackout on panel.

Evaluate: "Students" learned to match each of seven
                             three-digit binary numbers with any of
                             twenty-one possible combinations with good
                             accuracy (less than five errors per hundred
                             trials). However, it took hundreds of
                             thousands of trials to learn.
                             Note: "Students" in this experiment were
                             chimpanzees. These animals did not learn ab-
                             stract concepts but responded to specific
                             stimuli. This study gives additional hope for
                             teaching the mentally retarded to achieve full
                             potential.

Scientific Application[2]

Pinpoint:	*Talking, standing, blurting out, noisy inattention, turning around.* (Ten children—five different classrooms. Ages 6 years 8 months to 10 years 6 months. Teachers recommended most severe problem children in class.)
Record:	Trained observers recorded inappropriate social behavior for six weeks. Average inappropriate behavior was 72%.
Consequate:	Teachers: (1) made classroom rules explicit; (2) ignored behaviors which interfered with learning or teaching unless dangerous; (3) used withdrawal of approval as punishment; (4) gave praise and attention to behaviors which facilitated learning; and (5) attempted to reinforce prosocial behaviors *incompatible* with inappropriate social behaviors.
Evaluate:	Average inappropriate behavior decreased from 72% to 19.5% over an eight-week period. Note: Participating teachers were given a workshop in behavior modification during the experiment. Opportunities for each teacher to see daily observation graphs probably helped to increase effectiveness of the procedures.

Scientific Application[3]

Pinpoint: *Vandalism.*
                                   (7th grade)

Record: Seven students wrote on or destroyed: (1)
                                   desks, (2) walls, and (3) school equipment.

Consequate: (1) Desks—students sanded and revarnished
                                   damaged desks, plus two others. (2) Walls—
                                   students washed *entire* wall. (3) School equip-
                                   ment—students contributed double financial
                                   value. All work strictly supervised and com-
                                   pleted to satisfaction of teacher. Thereafter,
                                   students responsible for property upkeep,
                                   regardless of who caused damage. Parents *not
                                   allowed* to contribute to restitution in any
                                   manner.

Evaluate: Vandalism eliminated. Students' supervision of
                                   school property established. Note: This is per-
                                   haps one of the oldest and most effective
                                   discipline procedures.

Professional Application

Pinpoint:	*"Love note" passing—boy-girl talking.* (11th grade, biology class)
Record:	Five intercepted notes in one week (three innocuous—two vulgar). Twenty incidents of talking during one class period.
Consequate:	Friday field trip privilege contingent upon "no more talking or letter writing."
Evaluate:	Friday field trip denied two consecutive weeks—given third week after talking and letter writing stopped. Note: Field trips were continued throughout year. However, trips were subsequently denied four times for talking—sometimes students forget.

Professional Application

Pinpoint: *Increases in sentence speaking.*
                     (3rd grade boys, thirty; 3rd grade girls,
                     twenty-eight.
                     6th grade boys, twenty-one; 6th grade girls,
                     twenty;
                     10th grade boys, twenty; 10th grade girls,
                     thirty)

Record: Each child verbalized sixty sentences during
                     individual session.

Consequate: Students instructed to begin sixty sentences
                     with pronoun of choice. Researcher com-
                     mented "good" *only* after sentences starting
                     with the pronoun "I." No comment after any
                     others.

Evaluate: Number of sentences beginning with "I" in-
                     creased significantly.
                     Note: This study demonstrated effectiveness
                     of simple approval. However, the study also
                     indicated that the sex of a teacher may also
                     be a factor in effectiveness of approval.
                     Adolescent girls responded to praise from the
                     male researcher (first-year medical student) to
                     a greater extent than did adolescent males.
                     With *younger* students, the *boys* began more
                     sentences with "I," indicating a same-sex
                     preference for younger children.

Scientific Application[4]

Pinpoint: *Disruptive classroom behavior.*
         (9-year-old boy)

Record: Disruptions recorded by teacher.

Consequate: Disruptive behaviors ignored; appropriate behavior rewarded. Boy kept after school for extreme deviations and sent home on later bus. This put child with students he did not know and withdrew peer attention. Correct behaviors reinforced by teacher praise and peer-approval (continuously in beginning, more infrequently later on). Also, job of blackboard monitor followed appropriate behavior.

Evaluate: Disruptive behaviors initially *increased* as pay-off withdrawn. After initial rise, maladaptive behaviors progressively *decreased* and were eliminated by end of third week.

Scientific Application[5]

Pinpoint:	*Chewing-gum vandalism.* (8th grade, Special Education class)
Record:	Five (average) gum wads under each desk. Gum wrappers observed on floor (six-ten daily).
Consequate:	Gum privilege extended with admonition to "be responsible."
Evaluate:	Six (average) gum wads under each desk. Gum wrappers on floor (eight-eleven daily). **If at first you don't succeed?**
Consequate II:	Group gum chewing Monday, Wednesday, Friday contingent upon rules: Rule 1. "If an individual is caught chewing Tuesday and Thursday, individual will lose privileges of chewing gum for one week. He must also clean five wads from under desk." Rule 2. "If more than two wrappers are found on floor Monday, Wednesday, or Friday, entire class loses gum chewing privileges for one day."
Evaluate II:	After three weeks all gum wads removed from under all desks. Two wrappers Monday, Wednesday, and Friday observed on floor. Note: If contingency would have stipulated *no* gum wrappers, probably all wrappers would have been put away.

Professional Application

Pinpoint:	*Disruptive behavior.* (large class)
Record:	Absolute cacaphony. *No* recording able to take place.
Consequate:	Many children removed from class until class size became manageable. Teacher planned specific assignments and scheduled consequences. After small number of children brought under control, one child at a time added to class. Procedure started with limited number of children during special period while others normally out of room—later extended to entire day.
Evaluate:	Teachers indicated procedure very effective. Note: Teachers also stated that initial control of the *entire* group was absolutely impossible.

Professional Application

Pinpoint: *"Boredom."*
                                   (10th grade, Spanish)

Record: Lack of enthusiasm for subject-matter acqui-
                                   sition —only two of twenty-three assignments
                                   completed in two-week period.

Consequate: Friday football game instituted: teams chosen,
                                   rules established, points, yards, substitutions,
                                   etc., developed for correct *academic* responses.
                                   Game played on blackboard with losing team
                                   providing "treat" for winners.

Evaluate: "Enthusiasm replaced boredom"—*all* assign-
                                   ments completed by second Friday.
                                   Note: Any game may be used for any subject
                                   matter. It is best to choose a game specifically
                                   appropriate to the general outside interests of
                                   the student age group.

Professional Application

Pinpoint:	*"Off task" individual study.* (7th grade, Special Education class)
Record:	Completion of work taking longer each day and extending into next period. (Average time increase—twenty minutes by end of third week.)
Consequate:	All water-drinking privileges made contingent upon finishing work on time. Water-drinking frequency increased considerably but functioned as a positive reward.
Evaluate:	Increase in finished work in allotted time by end of fourth day. Note: The contingent delivery of other materials previously not associated with proper study (crayons, pencils, colors) was later introduced to reward other academic behaviors.

Professional Application

Pinpoint:

School failure.
(16-year-old boy)

Record:

Failed all academic subjects first half of year. Parents and teachers unable to "motivate studying."

Consequate:

School counselor developed system with parents' cooperation. Every teacher signed individual *daily progress report* (one small sheet) after each class. Decision of signing for appropriate social and academic behaviors based on teacher's criteria. Allowance, social engagements, car privileges contingent upon number of signatures earned each day.

Evaluate:

Better grades. C+ average attained for last six-week period of same year.
Note: Many parents offer rewards for good grades but cannot find a way to cut down the time interval so that rewards are meaningful in motivating the student. A complete academic term is very long for a student who cannot exhibit correct study patterns throughout one day.

Professional Application

Pinpoint: *Nail biting.*
(individual students—ages 6, 8, 9, 17)

Record: *Excessive nail biting*
(one instance of physical damage)

Consequate: *Negative practice.* Students practice *inappropriate* behavior at specific times (e.g., 8:00 for five minutes) in front of mirror. Parent or teacher delivered disapproval responses during nail biting sessions—"Doesn't that look terrible? Do you want people to see you bite your nails like that?" Children instructed to move hand up and down, biting repeatedly. During first session two children cried and wanted to stop.

Evaluate: Nail biting ceased after six-ten sessions. Note: Behaviors such as nail biting are behaviors whose frequency has made them habitual. Concentrated negative practice probably serves as a stimulus by which the child begins to discriminate. The child learns to "think" as his hand starts to go up, and therefore inhibits himself. Negative practice has been used successfully in eliminating nose-picking, thumb-sucking, pubic scratching, tics, and other social improprieties.

Professional Application

Pinpoint: *Guffaw laughing.*
                     (10th grade, six boys)

Record: Teacher's instructions elicited loud laughing
                     from boys.

Consequate: Boys collectively taken out of room—brought
                     back individually in front of class as girls
                     applauded. Seating arrangements also changed
                     to place each boy among group of girls.

Evaluate: Guffaw laughing ended. Note: The same pro-
                     cedure of boy-girl seating was employed for
                     the entire student body during general assem-
                     blies, resulting in considerable decrease in cat-
                     calls and noise. It also helped boy-girl
                     socialization.

Professional Application

Pinpoint:

Fear in young children.
(separate studies concerning six hundred children, infants and school age)

Record:

Overt signs of fear exhibited whenever children confronted fearful situations. Procedures reported from parent interviews and classified according to effectiveness.

Consequate:

Following procedures reported effective by parents: (1) *Incompatible response.* Feared object or situation gradually introduced into child's presence while child engaged in fun activity; (2) *Gradual approach.* Child led by degrees (over a number of days) to come closer and closer to feared object or participate in feared activity; (3) *Modeling.* Feared activity or object made readily accessible to child while other children participated enjoyably.

Evaluate:

Incompatible responses, gradual approach, and *modeling* eliminated about 85% of children's fears, according to parents. Note: The following procedures were *not* successful: disapproval, social ridicule, scolding, verbal appeals, punishment, forcing child to participate or changing the child's activity whenever he was afraid. When any fearful situation is forced upon a child, fear is *increased.*

Scientific Application[6]

Pinpoint: *Low-level skill achievement.*
                             (9th grade, industrial arts class)

Record: No evidence of completed individual project
                             or increased skills after fourth week of term.

Consequate: Teacher continually threatened students with
                             failing final grades for lack of industry.

Evaluate: Only *one* student of eight finished final
                             project.
                             Note: Anxiety increases were observed during
                             the last few days of class, as students fran-
                             tically tried to finish projects. One boy was
                             cut with a handsaw two days before term
                             ended. Students complained that they tried,
                             but "didn't really know what the teacher
                             wanted." This represents a situation where the
                             teacher "did not start where the student is."
                             Thus, threats of disapproval did not produce
                             constructive behavior; rather, threats produced
                             anxiety and subsequent physical harm.

Professional Application

Pinpoint:	*"Off-task" during individual seatwork.* (six elementary students, one first grader, two third grade classmates, three other classmates).
Record:	Observers recorded 40% study time (percentage of on-task ten-second intervals) during thirty minutes of seat work. (Number of observations varied from seven to fifteen days.)
Consequate:	Observers helped teachers by holding up small colored papers when children were studying. Teachers would go to the student and use verbal, facial, and contact approval.
Evaluate:	Study behavior increased to average 75% for the six students.
Consequate II:	Teachers stopped giving approval to study behavior.
Evaluate II:	Average study behavior dropped to 34%.
Consequate III:	Teachers again gave approval when observers signaled.
Evaluate III:	Study behavior increased to 73%.
	Note: Most teachers' attention to problem children was for nonstudy behavior during Record phase. It was also reported that classrooms were initially well controlled with a few students who did not stay on-task. Teacher approval was made contingent through observers' signals which later proved to be unnecessary and the cues were eliminated. The cues were initially used to make the teachers aware of contingencies.

Scientific Application[7]

Pinpoint: *Noisy transition changing classes.*
                           (8th grade)

Record: Length of time, after bell rang, students took
                           to be in seats steadily increased to eight
                           minutes.

Consequate: "Record party" contingent upon all students
                           being in seats before final bell. One "pop"
                           record (brought by students) played during
                           Friday's class for each day all students in seats
                           before final bell.

Evaluate: Extended record parties by end of third week.
                           Note: A decrease in other maladaptive
                           responses was observed when one record was
                           deducted from "Friday's list" for antisocial
                           behavior from any student.

Professional Application

Pinpoint:	*Rowdiness.* (6th grade)
Record:	Average of eight disruptive behaviors during each ten-second observation.
Consequate:	Students allowed play break with admonition: "I will let you play now if you promise to work afterwards." Students promised they would.
Evaluate:	*In*effective study behavior (nine-twelve average for ten-second intervals). Note: Rewards must come *after the fact.* After correct "work precedes play" contingency has been established, sequencing may then become effective (i.e., work, play, work, play, work, etc.).

Professional Application

Pinpoint: *Crawling.*
                             (Nursery school, girl 3.4 years)

Record: Girl spent 75% of time (observed two weeks)
                             in off-feet position. Also avoided contacts
                             with other children and adults.

Consequate: Nursery school teachers *ignored* girl when not
                             standing; approached, praised, displayed in-
                             terest when girl on feet. Disapproval tech-
                             niques such as anger, shame, disgust, or dis-
                             appointment not used.

Evaluate: Girl stood 75% of time during first week.
                             During second week, up as much as other
                             children.

Consequate II: Contingencies reversed. Teachers approved *off-*
                             feet behavior.

Evaluate II: First day of reversal, girl off-feet 75% of time;
                             second day 81.9%.

Consequate III: Return to praise for standing.

Evaluate III: First hour of first day, on-feet 75.9%; first
                             hour of second day 62.7%, by second hour
                             100%. *No relapses observed.* Note: The reader
                             may be wondering why one would deliberate-
                             ly produce inappropriate behavior in a stu-
                             dent. In a research study, the experimenter
                             must determine that a particular reinforcer is
                             really causing a specific effect. In this case the
                             reinforcer was praise—the effect, standing.
                             When a teacher is "sure" what produces a
                             desired change in the classroom, this may be
                             enough. However, the scientist must be cer-
                             tain. The reversal technique will be noted
                             repeatedly in scientific investigations.

Scientific Application[8]

Pinpoint:	*Homework study.* (high school, 17-year-old girl)
Record:	Grades monitored for one semester. Average grade D—with frequent failures.
Consequate:	Flash cards developed by student to assist study in history, civics, Latin. Meals contingent (except breakfast) upon success in responses to cards.
Evaluate:	Within eight weeks grades rose from D to a B-average. Note: Researchers noted the flash cards may have been reinforcing instead of the food. However, a follow-up at a later semester indicated grades had returned to a D average. Obviously, cards or grades alone were not sufficient rewards for this girl. Motivation must come from without before it gets "in." The question of how long it takes for motivation to "get in" for each individual is not known. However, it would appear that even constant rewarding is better than constant failure.

Scientific Application[9]

Pinpoint:	*Physical aggression.* (nursery school, twenty-seven 3-4-year-old boys)
Record:	Physical aggression frequency totaled 41.2, verbal aggression 22.8, with total 64.0 (one week observation).
Consequate:	Teachers ignored aggression and rewarded co-operative and peaceful behaviors (interfered only when bodily harm was likely). Approval techniques replaced reprimands.
Evaluate:	Total aggressive behaviors decreased—64 to 43.4. (Physical aggression 41.2 to 26.0; verbal aggression 22.8 to 17.4.)
Consequate II:	Following initial consequate, researchers told teachers experiment completed. However, observations again recorded three weeks later.
Evaluate II:	After experimenters left, teachers not as consistent. Total number aggressive responses increased 43.4 to 51.6. Physical aggression increased 26.0 to 37.8. However, verbal aggression decreased 16.4 to 13.8. (Teachers found it harder to ignore fighting than to ignore verbal threats.)
Consequate III:	Consequate I reinstated.
Evaluate III:	Total aggression decreased 51.6 to 25.6. Physical aggression decreased 37.8 to 21.0; verbal aggression 13.8 to 4.6. Note: This study substantiates the necessity of *absolute consistency.*

Scientific Application[10]

Pinpoint:	*Aggressive hitting.* (preschool boys, private kindergarten)
Record:	Teacher complained boys went "out of control" during outside play periods (five children hurt in one week).
Consequate:	Large punching bag dummy with red nose installed on playground.
Evaluate:	No noticeable decrease in human hitting—six children hurt during week. Dummy punched frequently, especially in nose. (Actually, boys fought each other to take turns at dummy.)
Consequate II:	Punching dummy removed. Individual boys isolated for duration of play period when observed hitting another child.
Evaluate II:	After five days (seventeen isolations), hitting completely eliminated. Note: Hitting, like other behavior, is *learned.* It is not a mystical entity deep inside everyone's system waiting to be released. The more children are reinforced for hitting, the more they will hit. Some people even develop a curious "self-fulfilling prophecy" in this regard. They sincerely believe that if they could just hit something they would feel much better. Thus, when frustrated, they hit something and, sure enough, they feel better.

Professional Application

Pinpoint: *Arithmetic achievement.*
                               (6th grade, thirteen boys)

Record: Assignments completed during arithmetic
                               period preceding recess averaged 4.2 (approxi-
                               mately nine incomplete assignments). Recess
                               activity closely observed. All boys played
                               100% of the time during two-week period.

Consequate: Boys told if assignments not completed, they
                               could not go out to recess.

Evaluate: Only four incidents of recess participation
                               were earned during the next week (three for
                               one child). Arithmetic assignment completion
                               did *not* increase following application of con-
                               tingency.

Consequate II: All boys instructed to work through recess
                               and *denied* recess privilege. However, each boy
                               allowed five minutes' play in gym after
                               finishing two arithmetic problems correctly.

Evaluate II: Completed arithmetic assignments increased to
                               nine by end of first week. By Tuesday of
                               second week, all thirteen boys turned in
                               assignments every day. After three weeks,
                               accuracy reached an average of 80%.
                               Note: This application represents a discrimina-
                               tion many teachers fail to make. If the period
                               of work is too long, the child cannot see the
                               immediate rewards for his academic work;
                               thus, behavior does not improve. It was ap-
                               parent to the teacher that these thirteen boys
                               (all retarded in arithmetic) really enjoyed
                               recess. The teacher used recess contingently,
                               but it did not work. The time span of work
                               without reward for these particular boys was
                               too long. When the rewarding activity was
                               given following a short period of work, they
                               all produced—even though regular recess was
                               denied. To keep the boys coming back from

the gym rapidly, the teacher occasionally rewarded them immediately with another period in the gym for prompt return. By the end of the second week, all boys were running back from the gym to work again. When using activities as rewards, it is important to pay very close attention to "structuring activities in time."

Professional Application

Pinpoint: *Striking children with objects.*
                             (9-year-old boy)

Record: Boy hit other children five times during four
                             free-play periods.

Consequate: Adult assigned in vicinity. Boy praised and
                             given donut when playing properly, although
                             when boy hit someone, supervisor instructed
                             to hit him back with same object. During
                             second supervised play period, boy hit another
                             child in head with plastic baseball bat.
                             Immediately, supervisor picked up bat and hit
                             boy. Explanation to child: "When people are
                             hit, it hurts."

Evaluate: Boy never observed hitting another child.
                             Note: This boy had been characterized as
                             "having no conscience." Perhaps it would be
                             more accurate to say that he did not realize
                             the consequences of his own actions regarding
                             pain.

Professional Application

Pinpoint: *Excessive dawdling.*
(5th grade)

Record: Three to five minutes to get "on-task" in individual study. (Average over eight days.)

Consequate: Teacher instituted multiple divergent token systems. Some children received paper money which bought "surprise gifts" at end of day. Other children received candies on various time interval schedules. Some children accumulated points written in notebooks. Reinforcers changed constantly. Varying token reinforcers "stimulated interest and created mode of excitement in classroom."

Evaluate: Individual dawdling decreased to approximately thirty seconds (average three days). Note: Expectation level increased general classroom excitement toward goal achievement (receiving tokens), which was later modified by stretching the time interval using only exchange tokens. If students have previously been on a single token system, sometimes it is wise to alter the routine.

Professional Application

Pinpoint:	*Isolate behavior.* (girl, age 4.3)
Record:	Varied repertory of well-developed skills pleased adults but did not gain child-child interactions. Observations during entire mornings by trained observers (one week) indicated: 10% child interaction, 40% adult interaction, 50% isolate.
Consequate:	Maximum adult attention for child interaction. *No* attention for isolate behavior or adult interaction.
Evaluate:	Over six days child interaction increased to 60%, adult interaction decreased to 20%, time spent alone 20%.
Consequate II:	Contingencies withdrawn.
Evaluate II:	Child interaction *decreased* to 20%, adult *increased* to 40%, isolate 40%.
Consequate III:	Contingencies reestablished. Attention for interaction with children. Child interaction increased to 60%, adult decreased to 25%, 15% isolate. Note: Follow-up observations showed girl to be maintaining the increased ratio of child interaction.

Scientific Application[11]

Pinpoint: *High noise level—lunchroom.*
(grade school)

Record: Generalized noise (talking) at high level observed by principal. Other maladaptive behaviors developing, i.e., hitting, screaming, not staying at table until finished.

Consequate: Sound-activated switch (inexpensive circuit breaker device) connected to lights in lunchroom. When noise reached preset level (first day, 80 decibels; second day, 70 decibels, etc.), lights went off. When noise dropped, lights came on.

Evaluate: Selected noise levels maintained without *any* instruction. Children learned quickly to stay just beneath sound level setting.
Note: A similar device is available that can be set at any intensity level. This device sounds a shrill pitch until noise stops. Mechanical disciplinarians are absolute and effective. More important, they free a teacher's time for more productive interactions.

Professional Application

Pinpoint: *Disruptive behaviors.*
                             (3rd grade, Adjustment class, seventeen 9-
                             year-olds)

Record: Normal kinds of reinforcers (praise, grades)
                             ineffective. Compliments from teacher resulted
                             in children making faces at each other. Eight
                             most disruptive children observed for one
                             hour and forty minutes three days per week.
                             Daily average of inappropriate behavior during
                             three-week observation was 76% (range
                             61%-91%).

Consequate: Reward program instituted for afternoon
                             hours while activities included stories, records,
                             arithmetic instruction, and group reading. Re-
                             ward procedures explained to children every
                             day for one week prior to consequate. Small
                             notebooks taped to child's desk. Every twenty
                             minutes teacher gave each child a score from
                             1 to 10. Points exchanged for playthings at
                             end of one hour and forty minutes during
                             first three days; days five through nine, points
                             exchanged after two days. During next fifteen
                             days, delay stretched to three-day period; for
                             last twenty-four days, four-day delay. In ad-
                             dition to individual rewards, *group* points
                             earned and exchanged for popsicle party end
                             of each week.

Evaluate: Average inappropriate behavior decreased from
                             76% to 10% (range 3%-32%). Decline evident
                             for every child.
                             Note: The total cost for entire program was
                             $80.67. Teacher's reports and observer's
                             records demonstrated profound difference in
                             this classroom. The teacher also indicated that
                             she had more time in which to teach. By
                             pairing verbal praise with dispensing of points,

the praise began to have a generalized effect even during the morning hours when the token system was not in operation.

Scientific Application[12]

Pinpoint: *Stuttering.*
                     (three adult males)

Record: Stuttering tabulated by analyses of two-minute intervals.

Consequate: Stuttering resulted in mild shock delivered to wrist.

Evaluate: Almost total reduction of stuttering. However, when shock removed, stuttering returned to original frequency.
                     Note: The use of shock as disapproval must be carefully controlled under appropriate supervision. This single scientific application (chosen from many) merely illustrates that the teacher has done only half the job when the inappropriate behavior is not replaced with appropriate behavior.

Scientific Application[13]

Pinpoint:	*Standing up, walking around.* (1st grade, forty-eight students, team-taught)
Record:	Average of 2.9 children out of seats during each ten-second interval. (291 children were counted [average] during twenty-minute period—twelve days.) Teachers told specific children to "sit down" an average of six times per twenty minutes. Whenever teacher told a child to sit down, the child did.
Consequate:	Teachers instructed to tell children who stood up without good reason to sit down (average once every minute).
Evaluate:	Amount of standing up *increased.* Each student sat down when told to sit down, but, overall, *more pupils stood up.* (Pupils standing per ten-second interval averaged 4.14.)
Consequate II:	Procedure reversed, i.e., children told to sit down only six times per twenty minutes.
Evaluate II:	Standing decreased to approximately original level (3.14 pupils standing per ten-second interval).
Consequate III:	To demonstrate that teachers' comments "caused" the children to stand up, teachers again told children up without good reason to "sit down" (average once every minute).
Evaluate III:	Standing up again increased to about same level as the first time teachers "paid attention" (3.94 per ten-second interval).
Consequate IV:	*Vicarious approval* introduced. Teachers praised good *sitting.* Whenever one child stood up or walked around, teacher "caught" a sitting student working diligently and praised the "good" child.

Evaluate IV:

Standing *decreased* (1.89 average).

Note: Praise delivered to individuals who were *not* standing was very effective in controlling the entire class. (What teacher hasn't noticed—thirty backs straighten when one child is complimented for sitting up straight and paying attention?) In this study the "good child" was used as a model for the group. ("Watch how quietly Susie gets her math counter!" "See how nicely Jim writes," etc.) Vicarious praise, however, was effective only for approximately thirty seconds. Even when 1st-graders "know the rules," it is necessary to deliver praise comments very regularly. It should be remembered that attention is extremely important to most children. Sometimes by paying attention to *inappropriate* behavior, you probably increase the very behavior you wish to eliminate.

Scientific Application[14]

Pinpoint: *Disruptive social talking.*
(junior high school, six girls)

Record: Talking recorded on sheet of paper taped to teacher's desk (77% of time, three days).

Consequate: Teacher explained to class that talking during study time interfered with completion of work assignments (this had been done before). Class discussed importance of rules for study, agreed something must be done, and suggested very extreme alternatives. Teacher then stated: "Anyone caught talking in class during study time must leave the room." Five girls sent out during next two days.

Evaluate: Eightfold *decrease* in talking followed four weeks of contingency.
Note: One caution in using this type of procedure should be mentioned. The technique of removing students from a classroom (isolation) is effective only when the classroom provides many positive consequences (i.e., the student would rather spend his time in the classroom than be isolated). The girls in this classroom were *very concerned* with receiving approval from one another as well as from the teacher; thus isolation was effective.

Professional Application

Pinpoint: *Disruptive behaviors—rest time.*
                             (1st grade, nineteen children)

Record: Average inappropriate behavior 54% (trained
                             observers ten days). Teacher gave praise or
                             reprimands twelve times during ten-fifteen
                             minute rest period.

Consequate: Teacher contingently praised appropriate
                             behavior, ignored disruptive behavior (twelve
                             praise comments per day—only two repri-
                             mands in eight-day observation).

Evaluate: Disruptive behavior averaged 32%.

Consequate II: Teacher reprimanded so no one except dis-
                             ruptive child could hear (eleven per day — no
                             praise seven days).

Evaluate II: Disruptive behavior averaged 39%.

Consequate III: Disapproval comments contingent on inappro-
                             priate behavior loud enough for entire class to
                             hear (fourteen per day; no approval for five
                             days).

Evaluate III: Disruptive behavior increased to an average of
                             53%.

Consequate IV: Teacher praised appropriate behavior, ignored
                             inappropriate behavior (five days — twelve
                             approval comments).

Evaluate IV: Disruptive behavior averaged 35%.
                             Note: In this scientific study the teacher
                             controlled disruptive behavior by praising and
                             reprimanding quietly. Loud reprimands
                             (yelling?) increased rather than decreased the
                             inappropriate behavior. A combination of ap-
                             proval for appropriate behavior and firm state-
                             ments to the individual offender often serves
                             to control young children very well. Quiet

reprimands eliminate the possibility of the other children paying undue attention to the misbehaving child.

Scientific Application[15]

Pinpoint: *Teaching contractual agreements.*
                                (9th grade, civics)

Record: Nothing.

Consequate: Beginning of term each student wrote contract
                                including amount of work to be completed
                                for special class project as well as evaluation
                                criteria for determining student's grade. In-
                                dividual contracts exchanged among students.
                                Entire class then chose a project and wrote
                                one contractual agreement determining indi-
                                vidual and collective responsibilities, including
                                penalties for "illegal" behaviors. Teacher
                                assumed role of interested bystander as stu-
                                dents pursued class project. Disputes during
                                course of project adjudicated in "class court"
                                (some students did not do their share of
                                work).

Evaluate: Effective learning judged by teacher on basis
                                of *ex post facto* essays written by students.
                                Note: It is interesting that the predominant
                                theme of most essays concerned "fairness."
                                Written contractual agreements are very effec-
                                tive for this age group and may concern any
                                cause-and-effect relationship between the
                                parties (teacher/student, parent/student). Con-
                                tracts specify contingencies ("If I do my work
                                you promise to pay me," etc.) and may be
                                used for individuals and/or groups. Exactly
                                the same benefits accrue from such written
                                contracts as from similar, more sophisticated
                                adult agreements.

Professional Application

Pinpoint:	*Overactivity in classroom.* (9-year-old boy, academic retardation)
Record:	Home and classroom observations determined frequency and categories of hyperactive behavior—talking, pushing, hitting, pinching, moving, tapping, squirming, handling objects, i.e., did not sit still.
Consequate:	A box, 6" x 8" x 5", equipped with counter and light, installed in classroom. Following ten seconds of appropriate behavior, light flashed, counter advanced, and boy received M & M or penny. Accumulated awards divided among classmates. Thus, other children received rewards for ignoring. Training session varied from five to thirty minutes; average rewards dispensed 60-100.
Evaluate:	Significant decrease in activity level (average decrease of 8.4 responses). Note: The peer group in this study was used to reward the deviant boy. Thus, the group began to have a positive effect upon him. Teachers can have an entire class help one or more children. Rewards may be given for both ignoring and paying attention. It is also suggested with *extremely* active children to: (1) use a stopwatch and start with as little as five seconds while counting to the child (verbal cues help the child perform in time); then reward immediately. Make sure the child does not get rewarded if he moves as much as an eyebrow. Gradually build the time sequence so child can remain still for thirty seconds or more; and (2) have the child practice the hyperactivity on purpose for five minutes a day to help the child discriminate between sitting still and moving.

Scientific Application[16]

Pinpoint: *Teaching beginning reading.*
                           (Ten research studies employing four hundred
                           children: retarded, slow readers, and un-
                           selected kindergarten and 1st grades.)

Record: Reading scores assessed prior to reading in-
                           struction.

Consequate: Programmed reading for periods of up to one
                           semester.

Evaluate: No tutored children failed to read with excep-
                           tion of one "normal" 1st grader and some (but
                           not all) children with I.Q.'s below 50. One
                           experiment showed relatively rapid acquisition
                           of reading vocabulary by simple pairing of
                           words with pictures. In another study, re-
                           tarded children taught reading vocabulary to
                           other retarded children with simple tutoring
                           program. In other research, sight-reading vo-
                           cabulary taught in sentence contexts to slow
                           readers, retarded, and normal children. Two
                           extension studies showed frequent alternation
                           of programmed tutoring and classroom teach-
                           ings more effective than less frequent alter-
                           nation. One study indicated reinforcement
                           proportion of approximately 20% more effec-
                           tive than higher levels.
                           Note: It appears that periodic withholding of
                           approval develops a "hope" which is more
                           effective than when the teacher reinforces all
                           the time. The interested teacher can find
                           literally hundreds of experiments in scientific
                           journals concerning the effects of various rein-
                           forcement schedules. The central issues related
                           to programmed instructions seem little dif-
                           ferent from any other teaching-learning se-
                           quence. One should begin where the student
                           is. Learning steps should be small, and ade-
                           quate reinforcement and feedback techniques

should be employed. Every teacher can individualize instructions and follow these systematic procedures.

Scientific Application[17]

Pinpoint:	*Noncooperation.* (11th grade, English, five boys)
Record:	No English assignments completed during two-week period. Students also refused to recite orally. Boys caught "shooting craps" in back of room.
Consequate:	All boys sent to principal's office and given a "good talking to" concerning classroom responsibilities and advantages of learning English.
Evaluate:	No change occurred in behavior. Boys became more noncooperative and began to mimic female teacher. Caught shooting craps twice during following week.
Consequate II.	Teacher began to praise every class member who cooperated in giving oral recitations from selected literature.
Evaluate II:	No change noted. Not one boy volunteered to participate in oral recitations. Teacher saw dice once but didn't catch boys in any games.
Consequate III:	Everyone who participated in oral recitations allowed to bring any book or magazine to class for thirty minutes of private reading.
Evaluate III:	One noncooperative boy brought a *Playboy* magazine to teacher after class and asked sarcastically: "If I read aloud from your book, can I read mine?" Teacher agreed. Next class session he did. Within four weeks all boys recited. Note: The teacher was also able to shift these boys' interest from *Playboy* to *Hot Rod,* and after four months to sophisticated sports magazines found in the school library. This

case demonstrates effective use of peer contingencies and approximations toward better literature through lack of censorship.

Professional Application

Pinpoint: *"Bad attitude."*
                           (1st-grade boy)

Record: Child continued maladaptive responses just a
                           little past point of instruction. Thus, when
                           teacher said, "Stop talking," he did but con-
                           tinued *almost* to point of being disobedient.
                           When teacher said, "Do not pick the flowers,"
                           he picked leaves. When she said, "Come here,"
                           he walked very slowly. When she said, "Quiet
                           down," he did—still slightly louder than the
                           group but not so loud as to receive punish-
                           ment. This child (like so many others) deli-
                           cately balanced upon the "edge of propriety."
                           Punishment seemed not quite warranted, and
                           reward seemed ridiculous.

Consequate: Teacher set up short lesson using *vicarious
                           modeling.* Three names not duplicated in class-
                           room were written on board. Class presented a
                           new work, *attitude.* Teacher paired names
                           with the new word:—"George has a *bad atti-
                           tude;* Sam has an *all right attitude;* Tommy
                           has a *good attitude.* When their teacher tells
                           these three boys, 'Let's all pick up the mess,'
                           George tries to get out of work or hides his
                           mess in the desk, Sam cleans up his own
                           mess—only his own—, but Tommy cleans up
                           his own mess and then helps other children."
                           The teacher talked through two such specific
                           examples, then let children say what they
                           thought George, Sam, and Tommy would do.
                           (Children are usually very correct in these
                           assessments, especially as they describe their
                           own problems.) Teacher made several praising
                           comments, stating: "I liked Tommy the very,
                           very best." She then asked problem boy
                           whom he would want for a friend. (The
                           teacher now had a word, *attitude,* that she
                           could use to describe this boy's behaviors in

specific and general contexts—"That's a good attitude, Cort.") She now began rewarding *good attitudes* instead of being frustrated at not being able to find responses to deal with this child.

Evaluate:

Child in question changed "attitude" when rewarded for proper verbal and motoric behavior.

Professional Application

Pinpoint: *Temper outbursts.*
                             (4-year-old boy—I.Q. recorded 72 and 80—
                             possible brain damage.)

Record: Frequency of objectionable behaviors varied
                             from 18 to 113 during sixteen one-hour
                             periods (sticking out tongue, kicking, yelling,
                             threatening to remove clothing, calling people
                             names, throwing objects, biting and hitting
                             self).

Consequate: Consequences applied by mother in home
                             two-three times per week for six one-hour
                             sessions. Researchers helped mother by giving
                             signals indicating: (1) she should tell her son
                             to stop what he was doing, (2) place him in
                             isolation for five minutes, or (3) give atten-
                             tion, praise, and affection.

Evaluate: Rate of objectionable behavior decreased
                             (range one-eight per session). Isolation used
                             four times; special attention given ten times.

Consequate II: No signals given; mother told to *"act as
                             before."*

Evaluate II: Objectionable behaviors increased, but ranged
                             well below original recordings (two-twenty-
                             four per session). It appeared mother
                             "learned." She reported more self-assurance,
                             increased attention, delivered firm commands,
                             and did not give in after denying a request.

Consequate III: Consequate I reinstated, except special atten-
                             tion for desirable play excluded.

Evaluate III: Objectionable behavior again *decreased*
                             (almost identical to Consequate I, ranging
                             two-eight per session).
                             Note: No contact was maintained with the
                             mother for twenty-four days after the ex-
                             periment. She was given no instructions as to

how to act and was given complete freedom
to use any technique she desired. Later,
three-session post contact check was made.
Even after this long delay, the behaviors considered objectionable were still very low. The
mother reported her child was well behaved
and less demanding. Isolation was used on the
average of once per week. The mother's attitude toward her son was also considered to be
more approving.

Scientific Application[18]

Pinpoint:

Academic failure.
(general—twelve students, different classrooms, age range 11-14)

Record:

Each student failed at least two academic subjects.

Consequate:

Individual work-play routines developed with consent of parents. Students given special after-school assignments (approximately thirty minutes). Work immediately checked by parents and points assigned. Points totaled each day to "buy" privileges and things (T.V. watching, outside peer playtime; two children received money; one child—supper; one student—Saturday hiking plus one T.V. program nightly; one student—time using "ham radio"). Time ratio for work-play approximately 4-1 in most cases. Thus, thirty minutes on-task work carried points worth two hours' activity or other reward.

Evaluate:

Eleven of twelve students improved (average increase 1.5 letter grades in four months); one 14-year-old ran away from home—this student entirely on money contingency—parents later admitted they began to pay him before, rather than after, study sessions, i.e., he was manipulating them, rather than vice versa.
Note: This program is effective, but demands absolute cooperation from parents. Many parents will respond to such a program when they: (1) admit their child has a problem, (2) have some confidence in the programmer (teacher/counselor), and (3) will be *honest* in dispensing rewards.

Professional Application

Pinpoint: *Classroom "out of control"*
(6th grade, thirty students, beginning teacher)

Record: Average classroom study rate during first hour 25% (four days).

Consequate: Teacher had two conferences with principal, wrote assignments on board, changed class seating arrangement, watched a helping teacher demonstration (study rate 90% during demonstration).

Evaluate: Average classroom study rate increased to 48% (thirteen days). Teacher averaged only 1.4 contingent approval comments per day to entire class during the period.

Consequate II: Teacher instructed in principles of contingent approval; contingent approval comments increased to average of thirteen per session.

Evaluate II: Average study rate rose to 67% (fourteen days).

Consequate III: Teacher discontinued contingent approval comments.

Evaluate III: Study behavior decreased steadily to 45% by sixth day.

Consequate IV: Teacher reinstated contingent approval averaging seventeen per session; decreased disapproval comments following nonstudy behavior.

Consequate IV: Study behavior increased average 77% (fourteen days)

Note: Three postexperimental observations indicated the study rates were being maintained at approximately the same level.

Scientific Application[19]

Pinpoint:

Academic fear.
(6th grade, social studies class, four girls)

Record:

Number of times girls volunteered during two-week period: zero. Only six questions answered when specifically directed toward them. Sociograms indicated girls isolates.

Consequate:

Activities developed with approval from teacher and classmates. Girls recited alone from assigned book, read passages for parents, who praised accomplishment, then read for teacher alone. Girls' voices recorded and positive verbal approval given by teacher for effective talking. Recording later played for entire class, who praised performance. Teacher also praised interaction with other children. Additionally, small groups of girls worked on projects. Each group started with one fearful girl and one girl who modeled appropriate behavior—number of students gradually increased.

Evaluate:

Volunteering in class increased from nothing to an average slightly below rest of class.
Note: These procedures are closely related to many learning situations where initial fear is gradually reduced by participating in the fear-producing activity (or approaching the feared objects) in small steps, receiving approval for behavior which is *incompatible* with avoidance.

Professional Application

Pinpoint:

Rehearsal effectiveness.
(high school band)

Record:

All stops by conductor constituted disapproval responses (traditional rehearsing procedure).

Consequate:

Band director marked two notated musical scores (equal difficulty and unfamiliar to band) with periodic pencil checks which divided musical phrases. During first score director stopped at each checkpoint, delivered *disapproval* responses regardless of performance quality. During second score, director stopped at checks and delivered specific compliments to performers.

Evaluate:

Compliments produced "a better performance and rehearsal attitude." Rehearsal time judged for equal performance level: disapproval = thirty-three minutes; approval = nineteen minutes.

Professional Application

Pinpoint: *Fighting during recess.*
                         (12-year-old boy)

Record: Teacher watched through window and re-
                         corded number of days boy hit other children
                         (four out of six days observed).

Consequate: Every time boy hit another child, taken into
                         principal's office and given one hard swat with
                         paddle.

Evaluate: Playground fighting *increased* after con-
                         sequences.

Consequate II: Procedures changed. Boy allowed talking pri-
                         vilege (five minutes) with principal every day
                         he behaved well on playground.

Evaluate II: Fighting behavior decreased to zero over four
                         weeks.
                         Note: Sometimes severe punishment can be
                         actually rewarding to a child. There are chil-
                         dren who associate any attention given by
                         authorities or adults as indications of ap-
                         proval. (This is not as absurd as it seems—
                         remember, we discipline those we care about.)
                         Some children receive only negative attention.
                         The application of approval following *good*
                         behavior changes this wrong association.

Professional Application

Pinpoint:	*Disruptive behaviors—talking, fighting, out of seat, throwing objects, noisy.* (7th grade, thirty students, beginning teacher)
Record:	Class met daily for forty minutes; had five-minute break followed by a forty-five minute session. Observation during first thirty minutes of session showed study behavior to average 47% (twenty-five days). Teacher gave contingent approval average of six times, disapproval for disruptive behaviors over twenty times per session.
Consequate:	Teacher increased attention to study behavior, decreased attention to "off-task" behavior. Contingent approval increased to nine times per session, disapproval to nine per session.
Evaluate:	Study behavior increased to average of 65% (six days). Noise level, disruptive behavior remained high.
Consequate II:	Teacher placed chalk mark on board when students disturbed class. Each mark reduced class break ten seconds (twenty-four marks canceled break).
Evaluate II:	Study behavior increased to 76% (twenty-four days). Noise dropped.
Consequate III:	Teacher eliminated disapproval contingencies (chalk marks). Attention to disruptive behavior was increased.
Evaluate III:	Study average dropped immediately; noise level increased.
Consequate IV:	All procedures reinstated.
Evaluate IV:	Study rate increased to 81% (maintained for remainder of study) Note: The overall noise level remained high even when there was a large gain in on-task

study behavior. It was necessary in this well-controlled scientific study to add a disapproval contingency (deprivation of break time for inappropriate behavior) before the classroom was brought under control. It should be emphasized that approval for good behavior can provide a positive atmosphere for learning even when disapproval procedures are employed.

Scientific Application[19]

Pinpoint: *Embarrassment.*
(10th-grade music, three girls)

Record: Self-evaluation indicated students possessed "no musical talent." Students refrained from individual singing, stating "My voice sounds funny" or "I cannot carry a tune."

Consequate: Twofold program to: (1) teach all students discrimination between (a) possessing ability and (b) performing before class, and (2) teach entire class role-playing to deliver approval feedback to "insecure students."

Evaluate: Students learned to participate in activities, even though they did not possess even moderate "talent." Class also taught to smile, nod heads, keep eye contact, and approvingly reinforce a terrible performance. Teacher played role of extremely poor singer while class learned to "put a performer at ease" by *not* responding to performer's fear and avoidance with fear and avoidance, but with approving reinforcement. Shy performers began participating regularly. One girl stated: "I have always known I've had a lousy voice, but now I love to sing."

Note: Students in upper grades who have a problem with embarrassment in relation to any activity have *learned* this embarrassment from someone. It is usually learned traumatically. For example, the young child sings and enjoys himself until one day he shockingly learns his voice sounds terrible, whereupon he stops singing. Unfortunately, some teachers do not understand the importance of teaching discriminations, and therefore continuously prepare many youngsters for disillusionment—some for catastrophe. Dedicated to well-intended censorship, many teachers pretend that no one is different from anyone. "Celia has only one arm, but in my classroom she has two, just like everyone else." "Fred has a lisp, but in my classroom we ignored his impediment." "Spencer is a Negro, but in my classroom everyone's skin is the same." It is unfortunate that these children must get out on the playground where other children do not censor: "Hey, Celia, what happened to your arm?" "Gosh, Fred, you talk funny." "Why are your hands white, Spencer?" Some children even make fun of these differences. Yet where can children learn to accept differences proudly and not make fun?—certainly not in a classroom where differences *do not exist.* Children can easily be taught discrimination of differences. Much more important, they can be taught *acceptance* and *respect* for differences. This learning, however, will not come from censorship.

Professional Application

Pinpoint:	*Unfinished assignments, bothering neighbors, playing in class.* (2nd grade, two boys referred by teacher)
Record:	Trained observers recorded average of 47% inappropriate behavior.
Consequate:	Teacher and class formulated rules. Rules repeated six times per day for two weeks.
Evaluate:	Little decrease in inappropriate behavior (average 40%). Note: Apparently just knowing (being able to repeat rules) is not effective.
Consequate II:	Teacher attempted to ignore inappropriate behaviors (teacher not entirely successful). Continued to repeat class rules every day.
Evaluate II:	Behavior worsened. Average inappropriate behavior for four observations 69%.
Consequate III:	Teacher praised prosocial behavior, repeated classroom rules, ignored inappropriate behavior.
Evaluate III:	Inappropriate behavior *decreased* (average of 20%). Combination of procedures effective in reducing inappropriate behavior.
Consequate IV:	Teacher instructed to act as she had in September. (Observers monitored entire year.)
Evaluate IV:	Inappropriate behavior increased same day teacher changed (averaged 38%).
Consequate V:	Rules, ignoring, and praise reinstated for remainder of school year.
Evaluate V:	Inappropriate behavior again decreased (averaged only 15% for last eight-week period). Note: Many teachers who believe they use more approval than disapproval do not (monitored by trained observers in classroom).

It is necessary to practice delivering responses and to give yourself time cues or cues written on material you are teaching. A mark on every page can remind you to "catch someone being good." It is interesting to note that one boy reported in this study was seen during the entire year by a professional counselor. This boy responded in the same way to consequences as did the other boy who was not seen. It would seem that the teacher is capable of handling many behavioral problems generally referred to counselors, if responses are well developed and applied contingently.

Scientific Application[20]

Pinpoint:

Lawbreaking.
(forty delinquent boys, average age 17.8, lower socioeconomic)

Record:

Average age at first arrest 13.5; average number arrests 8.2; total time incarceration 15.1 months. All boys arrested approximately same age, same nationality, equal number of months in jail, similar residence and religious preferences.

Consequate:

One group participated in consequences while "control" group did not. Boys not in school (most of them should have been) and met on street corners or other places of frequent occupancy. Each boy offered job and told researcher wanted to know "how teen-agers felt about things." Boys who participated rewarded with food, cokes, money, or tokens, depending upon each individual case. No punishment employed. Ossasionally, bonus rewards given for prompt arrival, proper verbalizations, and spontaneous interest.

Evaluate:

Groups compared three years later. Consequate group averaged 2.4 arrests, other group 4.7; average number of months in jail 3.5 for consequate group, 6.9 for other group. Illegal acts committed by consequate group less frequent and much less severe.
Note: In this particular study, consequences were *not* directed toward criminal behavior itself but represented an attempt to teach prosocial behavioral patterns. When a boy did not appear, the researcher would meet him out on the street and bring him to the lab. It is sometimes important for the teacher to go after a child and bring him where he should be. Any peer group such as the above juvenile group can exercise tremendous pressure to-

ward group conformity. Often peer rewards must be broken down or changed if the teacher is to succeed.

Scientific Application[21]

Pinpoint:	*Children manipulating parents.* (Three children and mothers trained in Child Development Clinic. A 6-year-old boy attempted to force parents to comply with his wishes. A 4-year-old boy considered excessively dependent at home, aggressive in nursery school. Another 4-year-old extremely stubborn in presence of mother but not with other adults.)
Record:	Each mother observed while interacting with son.
Consequate:	Mothers instructed: (1) in delivery of approval techniques, (2) to ignore inappropriate behavior, and (3) to respond with praise and affection for appropriate behavior. Mother A responded positively to child *only* when he did not attempt to force compliance. Mother B ignored child's dependency, responded approvingly to independent behavior. Mother C ignored oppositional behavior, responded to cooperate behavior. Later, Mother C instructed to isolate son in empty room for at least five minutes immediately following oppositional responses.
Evaluate:	First two boys' behavior improved markedly through mothers' attention to appropriate behavior and ignoring inappropriate responses. The third boy improved only after isolation. Note: This is a good example of differential treatment. The teacher should always remember that it is necessary to structure for each student. It should be noted that the use of punishment (isolation) was necessary for one child before improvement took place.

Scientific Application[22]

Pinpoint: *"Academic apathy."*
                       (11th grade, history, culturally disadvantaged)

Record: *No* evidence of *any* study behavior. Five days
                       constant harassment.

Consequate: Teacher left *all* books and teaching materials
                       home, sat at desk, looked at students, and
                       said nothing. Teacher continued procedure
                       day after day throughout *one entire week.*
                       Did not attempt to teach, control class, or
                       respond in any way.

Evaluate: During second week, two students timidly
                       brought books to class and asked what to do.
                       Teacher brought the two students to front of
                       room and began teaching. As days passed,
                       other students joined the small learning group.
                       By end of six weeks, every student involved.
                       Last seven students came into learning group
                       on same day.
                       Note: Much is said in education about stu-
                       dents establishing their own goals. The above
                       study is an excellent example of this concept
                       at its most basic level—for there is an infinite
                       distance between zero and one. Most students
                       do not know what their goals are. If they can
                       engage a teacher in battle, this often becomes
                       their goal. In the above case, students were
                       left with nothing. In time, they began to want
                       something, anything, even school work. Ignor-
                       ing takes a temporal patience many teachers
                       could well develop. Concerning the above stu-
                       dents, it should be noted that children who
                       live in extreme deprivation meet boredom and
                       apathy as an old friend. Perhaps more sophis-
                       ticated students would have developed goals
                       during this long period which excluded the
                       teacher entirely. When a teacher decides to
                       accept the contingencies (goals) of the student

peer group, he should do so in full knowledge of possible results. When speaking of "children establishing their own goals," it would seem wise for teachers to think this concept through. Most often this cliché indicates that the teacher *decides* to let children *decide* certain innocuous things. "You may choose any color you wish—you may not color on the wall." If, from the beginning, goals were left *entirely* to children, formal education would cease to exist. Knowledge and/or decisions cannot exist in a vacuum—"Tell me something you *do not know.*"

Professional Application

Pinpoint: *Dishonesty.*
                             (any classroom, anywhere)

Record: Three students caught cheating on first exam
                             of term.

Consequate: F grades assigned without explanation.

Evaluate: Same three students caught stealing "ditto
                             master" of second exam from typist's waste-
                             basket.

Consequate II: Each student asked to write short theme
                             stating reasons for cheating.

Evaluate II: Same three students caught cheating in falsi-
                             fying laboratory manual.

Consequate III: Students asked to prepare confessional speech
                             to be delivered before entire class. Parents of
                             two students strongly objected, stating such
                             treatment "would not only be a terrible exper-
                             ience, but damage children's reputations."
                             Principal received call from school board
                             member, after which students, parents, and
                             teachers instructed to meet in principal's of-
                             fice. At meeting, all students denied any
                             cheating whatsoever. Teacher presented first
                             themes of confession. Parents of one student
                             immediately placed her in private school.
                             Parents of second student persuaded principal
                             to allow daughter to withdraw from course.
                             Parents of third student did not come to
                             meeting. Teacher required this girl to make
                             confessional statement before class. She did,
                             but broke down crying before finishing. She
                             later told teacher it was the worst thing she
                             ever did in her life. Much later she told
                             teacher it was *second* worst thing she ever did
                             in her life.

Evaluate IV, V, VI, VII, etc.:

> *The science of behavior is predictable.* You
> know all three of these students, regardless of
> age, sex, or position.

Fictional Application

PART III

A Positive Approach

7

DEVELOPING
RESPONSES

The teacher has many reinforcers that may be used contingently in time to teach desired behaviors. However, merely reading, talking, and thinking about consequential responses does not produce optimum results. The development of effective responses takes *practice*. Consider for a moment the tremendous practice it takes for a poet to choose the precise word, for a musician to turn a beautiful phrase, for an actor to deliver an effective line. Practice in developing responses cannot be overemphasized. Just talking to yourself while looking into a mirror is very effective. A tape recorder can also be valuable in developing response skills. At first you will notice some tension—you will feel awkward and perhaps a little childish. Nevertheless, practice. A good place to start is with the words "thank you." Practice saying "thank you" with as many inflections as possible—from extreme sarcasm to sincere appreciation.

If one desires to express a sincere feeling, one must make sure the real intent will be expressed. Those people whom we consider warm and sensitive are people who have developed great skill in expression. Most often, expressions are not overtly practiced; yet all teachers (having been often misunderstood) should be sure to communicate their thoughts and feelings most effectively. Considering all the time we spend in front of the mirror on physical appearances, is it not incongruous we do not use some of this time to develop effective personal responses? After patient practice in role playing, the teacher will begin to notice exciting new skill in the development of responses. Sometimes a teacher may choose to practice with another person who desires to be helpful in giving the teacher appropriate feedback.

Other than subject matter itself, responses available to the teacher may be classified in five categories: (1) words (spoken-written), (2) physical expressions (facial-bodily), (3) closeness (nearness-touching), (4) activities (social-individual), and (5) things (materials, food, playthings, awards). The following lists have been developed as possible *approval* models for the teacher. The teacher should select and develop those reinforcers deemed usable as specific behavioral contingencies for the age and grade level of students involved. Start with one or two responses, develop thoroughly, and evaluate in the classroom before developing others.

Approval Responses

Words Spoken: Approval

Words

Yes	Correct
Good	Excellent
Neat	That's right
Nice	Perfect
O.K.	Satisfactory
Great	How true
Fascinating	Absolutely right
Charming	Keep going
Commendable	Good responses
Delightful	How beautiful!
Brilliant	Wonderful job!
Fine answer	Fantastic!
Uh-huh	Terrific!
Positively!	Swell
Go ahead	Beautiful work
Yeah!	Tasty
All right	Marvelous!

Nifty	Exciting!
Exactly	Pleasant
Of course	Delicious
Cool	Fabulous!
Likeable	Splendid
Wonderful	Well-mannered
Outstanding work	Thinking
Of course!	

Sentences

That's clever
I'm pleased.
Thank you.
I'm glad you're here.
That's a *prize* of a job.
You make us happy.
That shows thought.
We think a lot of you.
You're tops on our list.
That's good work.
Remarkably well done.
You're very pleasant.
That shows a great deal of work.
Yes, I think you should continue.
A good way of putting it.
I like the way ___(name)___ explained it.
That is a feather in your cap.
You are very friendly.
That's an excellent goal.
Nice speaking voice.
That's a nice expression.
It is a pleasure having you as a student.
That's interesting.
You make being a teacher very worthwhile.
That's sweet of you.
Well thought out.
Show us how.
You're doing better.

You are improving.

You're doing fine.

You perform very well, ___(name)___ .

That's very good, ___(name)___ .

I'm so proud of you.

I like that.

This is the best yet.

That's the correct way.

That's very choice.

You do so well.

You're polite.

Thinking!

Relationships

Nice things happen to nice children.

That is very imaginative.

You are worthy of my love.

That will be of great benefit to the class.

I admire it when you work like that.

That is original work.

I appreciate your attention.

You've been a fine credit to your class.

I commend your outstanding work.

We are proud to honor your achievement.

That was very kind of you.

You catch on very quickly.

Obedience makes me happy.

That deserves my respect.

You demonstrate fine ability.

That is clear thinking.

You should be very proud of this.

That was nice of you to loan her your _____.

I wish you would show me and the class how you got such an interesting effect.

I like that—I didn't know it could be done that way.

Permission granted.

That's a good job—other children can look up to you.

Let's watch him do it.

He accepts responsibility.
That *was* a good choice.
Show this to your parents.
I know how you feel—should we continue?
I'm happy your desk is in order.
Why don't you show the class how you got the answer?
That's a good point to bring up, ___(name)___ .
I agree.
Let's put this somewhere special.
I'd like this in my own house.
My, you have a nice attitude.
Now you're really trying.
Keep working hard, ___(name)___ .
You've improved.
Your work appears so neat.
You're a good person.
If at first you don't succeed, try, try again.
Thinking!

Words and Symbols Written: Approval

Bravo!	Good work
Improvement	↫
Fine	Correct
Good	+
Neato	Satisfactory
Very good	Nicely done
O.K.	Very concise
Passing	Complete
*	A, B, C, D
X	Enjoyable
✓	Excellent
Thoughtful	Outstanding
100%	☞
Good paper	[Colored pencil markings]
Very colorful	Superior
☺	Congratulations
Well done	Yeh
Great	Show this to your parents.

Wow!	[Honor rolls]
A-1	For display
Perceptive	[Rubber stamps]

Rules

In formulating rules, remember to:

1. Involve the class in making up the rules.
2. Keep the rules short and to the point.
3. Phrase rules, where possible, in a positive way. ("Sit quietly while working," instead of "Don't talk to your neighbors.")
4. Remind the class of the rules at times *other* than when someone has misbehaved.
5. Make different sets of rules for varied activities.
6. Let children know when different rules apply (work-play).
7. Post rules in a conspicuous place and review regularly.
8. Keep a sheet on your desk and record the number of times you review rules with class.

Expressions: Approval

Facial

Looking	Widening eyes
Smiling	Wrinkling nose
Winking	Blinking rapidly
Nodding	Giggling
Grinning	Whistling
Raising eyebrows	Cheering
Forming kiss	Licking lips
Opening eyes	Smacking lips
Slowly closing eyes	Pressing lips affirmatively
Laughing (happy)	Rolling eyes enthusiastically
Chuckling	

Bodily

Clapping hands	Grabbing
Raising arms	Bouncing

Shaking fist
Signaling O.K.
Cocking head
Skipping
Rubbing stomach
Thumbs up
Shaking head
Jumping up and down
Shrugging shoulders

Dancing
Stroking motions
Opening hands
Flipping head
Taking a fast breath
Expansive movements of hands
Hugging self

Circling hand through air (encouragement to continue)
Hand/finger to face, eyebrows, eyes, nose, ears, mouth, cheek, lips, hair, forehead

Closeness: Approval

Nearness

Nearness concerns physical proximity and ranges from geographical separation—through noticeable contact—to embracing
Interacting with class at recess
Eating with children
Sitting on desk near students
Sitting within the student group
Standing alongside
Walking among students
Gently guiding
Pausing—while transferring objects

Touching

Hand on hand
Ruffling hair
Touching head
Patting head
Pinching cheek
Pinching chin
Touching nose
Patting back

Retying sashes
Walking alongside
Combing hair
Tying shoes
Quick squeeze
Dancing
Rubbing back of neck
Gently raising chin

Patting shoulder
Touching arm
Straightening clothes
Hugging
Touching hand
Shaking hands
Squeezing hand
Patting cheek
Nudging
Helping put on coats

Leaning over
Touching hurt
Kissing a hurt
Putting face next to child
Tweaking nose
Tickling
Cupping face in hands
Gentle pull at hair
Running finger down person's nose
Guiding with hand

Activities and Privileges: Approval

Individual

Leading student groups
Representing group in school activities
Displaying student's work (any subject matter)
Straightening up for teacher
Putting away materials
Running errands
Caring for class pets, flowers, etc.
Collecting materials (papers, workbooks, assignments, etc.)
Choosing activities
Show and tell (any level)
Constructing school materials
Dusting, erasing, cleaning, arranging chairs, etc.
Helping other children (drinking, lavatory, cleaning, etc.)
Reading a story
Exempting a test
Working problems on the board
Answering questions
Outside supervising (patrols, directing parking, ushering, etc.)
Classroom supervision
Omitting specific assignments
First in line
Assisting teacher teach
Leading discussions

Making gifts
Recognizing birthdays
Grading papers
Special seating arrangements
Responsibility for ongoing activities during school holidays (pets, plants, assignments)
Decorating room
Presenting hobby to class
"Citizen of the Week" or "Best Kid of the Day"

Social

Movies
Decorating classroom
Presenting skits
Playing records
Puppet shows
Preparing for holidays (Christmas, Thanksgiving, Easter)
Making a game of subject matter
Outdoor lessons
Visiting another class
Field trips (subject matter)
Planning daily schedules
Musical chairs
Competing with other classes
Performing for PTA
Dancing
Going to museums, fire stations, courthouses, picnics, etc.
"Senior Sluff Day"
Participating in group organizations (music, speech, athletics, social clubs)
Talking periods
Recess or play periods
Early dismissal
Parties
Talent shows (jokes, readings, music, etc.)

Things: Approval

Materials

Storybooks
Pictures from magazines
Collage materials
Counting beads
Paintbrushes
Papier-mâché
Book covers
Crayons
Coloring books
Paints
Records
Flash cards
Surprise packages
Bookmarkers
Pencils with names
Seasonal cards (Valentines, birthday)
Pencil sharpeners
Subject-matter accessories

Pencil holder
Stationery
Compasses
Calendars
Buttons
Pins
Pictures
Musical instruments
Drawing paper
Elastic bands
Paper clips
Colored paper
Pets
Flowers
Classroom equipment
Chalk
Clay

Food

Jawbreakers
Lemon drops
Chocolate creams
Sugar cane
Cake
Candied apples
Lemonade
M & M's
Candy canes
Popcorn
Candy corn
Peanuts
Animal crackers

Milk
Sugar-coated cereals
Marshmallows
Apples
Gum
Crackers
Juices
Raisins
Lollipops
Candy kisses
Popsicles
Fruit
Crackerjacks

Ice cream

Soft drinks

Cookies

Candy bars

Potato chips

Life savers

Playthings

Toys

Perfume

Cartoons

Kaleidoscopes

Flashlight

Headdress

Rings

Striped straws

Kickball

Playground equipment

Tape recorders

Badges

Pins

Ribbons

Balls

Puzzles

Combs

Comics

Jump ropes

Balloons

Commercial games

Toy guns

Bats

Marbles

Toy jewelry

Jacks

Yo-yo's

Stamps

Whistles

Bean bags

Jumping beans

Wax lips and teeth

Masks

Straw hats

Banks

Address books

Fans

Silly putty

Toy musical instruments

Tokens (points)

Grab bag gifts

Birthday hats

Play dough

Dolls

Dollhouses

Makeup kits

Trains

Stuffed animals

Pick-up sticks

Cowboy hats

Boats

Blocks

Miniature cars

Snakes

Plastic toys (animals, indians, soldiers)

Money (play, real, exchangeable)

Class pictures

Household inexpensives (pots, coffee cans, all sizes of cardboard boxes)

Awards

Citations	Medals
Athletic letters	Cups
Plaques	Report cards
Pens	"Good Deed" charts

Subject-matter prizes (books, science hardware, subscriptions, etc.)

Disapproval Responses

The following lists gleaned from actual classroom observations contain *disapproval* responses. The teacher should study these lists carefully in order to achieve two important discriminations: (1) to recognize responses one may be unwittingly using and wish to eliminate or replace with incompatible approval responses, and (2) to plan carefully, responsibly, and cautiously the application of disapproval. The authors believe most of the following should *never* be used. *The teacher must discriminate.* Even a pleasant "hello" can be a scathing indictment if the tone and intensity of the voice causes that effect.

Words Spoken: Disapproval

This list includes naggings, sarcasms, bitternesses, dishonesties, and other ineffectual teacher responses whose angry delivery generally demonstrates that the *teacher,* not the student, has the problem.

Impractical
Be prompt
Work faster
Try to understand
Do your homework
Do your best
Unclear explanation
Don't you want to do things right?
It can't be that difficult
You're too slow
Stop talking

Behave
Pay attention
Don't
Wrong
Stupid
Be still
Follow directions
Think for a change
Use some thought
No, that's not what I said
Would you like to get paddled?
You don't understand because you don't listen!
If I find you chewing gum once more, you'll wear it on your nose
Be quiet and sit down
You're gutless
That's ridiculous
Meaningless
Absurd
Bad
Nonsense
Too vague
Try harder
Wrong
That's not right
Incorrect
Needs improving
Unsatisfactory
Poor
Undesirable
You should be ashamed
Useless
That's not clear
I dislike that
Don't be silly
That's terrible
What is this?
Is this something?
Quit making messes
Let's throw this away

That's not mature
I can't read anything you write
Haven't you learned how to spell?
Grow up
You're not doing as well as you used to
Horrible
Absolutely not!
Shh!
Stop
Listen to me
Maddening
Be quiet
Raise your hand
Stop that laughing
I'll have no more talking
Apologize now
Sloppy
Shut up!
I'll show you who's boss
One more time and you'll get it from me
Finish it now
No talking
I'll slap you silly
Look for the answer
Leave her alone
You march straight to the office
Keep your eyes on your own paper
You lack interest
I'll give you something to cry about
You *couldn't* have done worse
I do not like this
It's not up to requirements
I will not repeat it
I'm not telling you again
You're dull
That's ugly
You idiot
You're a laughingstock
It's hopeless for you

Why are you a fraidycat?
You're cheap
Snob
You're worthless
You're rude
Don't be crabby
You're disgusting
You little monster
Don't laugh at me
Cut it out
You're dumb
You're filthy
You naughty boy
Mock me and you won't hear the end of it
You're narrow-minded
That's childish
Simple Simon
No! No!! No!!!
You haven't applied yourself
Your work isn't acceptable
Get your mother to sign this bad paper
What do you mean you're not finished?
Stand up straight
Just try that once more
Anyone else!
Learn that!
You'd better get on the stick
So you're tardy again!
Speak when you're spoken to
Smart alec
You *must* be confused
I don't see your point
You know what happened the last time you did that
You do this over
You know better than that
Play fair
Don't cause problems
You're never dependable
That wasn't the right thing to do

Well, we'll never do this again
If you had a brain in your head, you wouldn't say that
Do it!
You think you're the only one here?
You're bad
Poor stupid oaf
Wrong again
You're doomed to failure
You're wrong all the time
You don't know anything
You make me sick
You're just an inadequate person
Impertinent
You're not thinking
You haven't been paying attention
Wipe that silly grin off your face
I guess I shouldn't expect any more from *you*
You're just plain boring
You have a dirty mind
Terrible! Terrible!
This isn't what *I* had in mind
You know that's wrong
Stupid nonsense
You'd *better* try harder
People never change

Expressions: Disapproval

Frowning
Curling lip
Lifting eyebrows
Looking at ceiling
Furrowing brows
Smirking
Lowering eyebrows
Shaking finger or fist
Wrinkling mouth
Squinting eyes

Staring
Wrinkling forehead
Nose in air
Puckering lips
Wrinkling nose
Pounding fists on table
Laughing
Shaking head
Turning away
Gritting teeth

Biting lips
Squinting eyebrows
Looking sideways
Closing eyes
Clicking tongue
Pushing mouth to one side
Pointing finger
Putting hand behind ear
Grimacing
Sniffing
Tightening jaw
Sticking out tongue

Twisting side of mouth
Cackling
Snickering
Turning head away
Letting out breath
Raising lips
Hissing
Fingers in front of lips
Nodding head (no)
Showing teeth
Pulling in bottom lip

Closeness: Disapproval

Closeness disapproval concerns corporal punishment and ranges from threatening approaches—through spankings—to severe physical beatings.

Activities and Privileges: Disapproval

Disapproval concerning activities and privileges constitutes various degrees of *deprivation*. Deprivation ranges from withholding of privileges—through isolation—to social incarceration.

Isolation
Ostracism
Silence periods
Sitting in corner
Staying after class
Writing misbehaviors
Standing in front of class
Leaving room
Extra work
Staying in from play
Being last to leave
Sitting in hall
Being sent to principal

Eating alone in lunchroom
Away from friends
Pointing out bad examples
Apologizing to class
Writing letters of apology
Bringing parents to school

Things: Disapproval

Concerning things, disapproval refers to inanimate materials that are damaging to the body: (1) intense noises (ear damage), (2) heat (fires and stoves), (3) chemicals (poisons), and (4) objects in motion (knives, cars, bullets, radiation). Obviously *none* of these should ever be used by the teacher (even washing a child's mouth out with soap can sometimes cause tissue damage).

Teaching and learning should be exciting and satisfying for both teacher and student. The innovative teacher has too many positive and effective resources available to resort to shoddy and punitive measures. Many experienced teachers state that almost all of their earlier punitive consequences could have been handled in a more positive manner. A teacher who truly cares will practice developing *positive* responses.

SUMMARY

Teaching—The art of <u>Discipline</u>

Many teachers leave the teaching profession because they have not developed effective techniques of classroom control and subject-matter presentation. While some teachers believe that discipline refers to a continuum from permissiveness through strictness, it is easily observed that this is not the case. Effective discipline insues from direct cause-and-effect relationships. Therefore, concepts such as spanking vs. loving, classroom freedom vs. dictatorship, expression vs. subjugation are extremely deceptive. Indeed, we discipline only those we love; social freedom can exist only within defined parameters; and self-expression, much like everything else, must be *learned*. The reason we discipline is to provide each child with behaviors necessary for individual productivity. Realizing that decisions determining what constitutes these basic behaviors (curriculum) are our responsibliity, we should structure wisely and not deceive ourselves by stating that children are deciding all things for themselves. When we teach children to think (i.e., establish values, decide), we should do so with the express purpose of insuring logical mediational sequencing and not use the euphemism "thinking" as a rationalization to eschew the responsibility of our job. Every teacher should initially realize that the teacher's primary responsibility is to acculturate the child. Teaching a child to spell, read, write, as well as to be well behaved, represents the *imposition* of social and educational values which do not originate with the student. The teacher who states, "Oh, but that's not what I mean," obviously needs some personal remediation in thought processes to differentiate between those aspects of life that are definitely mutually exclusive and those that are not. Every teacher should know precisely what decisions are to be the student's and what decisions are to be the teacher's. If a teacher accepts this responsibility and does not try to "give the problem away," children will acquire the basic learnings necessary to develop their own values. Regardless, one should realize that it takes a tremendous amount of courage to act on the basis of one's value orientation whether he be student or teacher.

Discipline — The way to <u>Learning</u>

The first aspect of discipline both socially and academically is to determine just *where the student is.* That is, to determine what behaviors currently are present and, therefore, to know precisely where to start. Regarding *academic learning* this involves structuring subject matter in easily attainable sequential steps beginning at the student's own level. In assessing *maladaptive responses* the deviant behavior itself is the foremost concern. An involved history of how the student got that way is both unproductive and unnecessary. Academic assessment should take several days, social assessment several minutes. All too often, knowledge concerning a terrible home life, bizarre past experiences, or personality test scores provides the opportunity for some teachers to give up on the child because the teacher discovers a "reason" for the deviant behavior. If students are not "motivated to learn," then motivation must be taught before the teacher should expect it to be internalized; it must come from without before it can be from within. Desire for learning (motivation) is taught by establishing *rewards* for learning, first extrinsically, later intrinsically. Realizing that at some point learning usually represents work, the teacher must stretch the ratio of previously established rewards to motivate students through the difficult times. This represents a process of partial reinforcement to teach for long-term goals, i.e., establish maturity.

Learning — The modification of <u>Behavior</u>

Learning necessitates experience, discrimination and association. Behavior modification is a process for structuring learning experiences to provide fine discriminations and correct associations. However, the teacher must deal with specified overtly demonstrable behaviors if the teacher expects to know what has been learned. It has been demonstrated that if a student knows precisely what is expected of him and he wants to do it, he probably will. Preparing expectancies for students necessitates the structure of goals. Instructional goals should represent definable overt responses which are realistic, manageable, and, above all, measurable. All behaviors, both social and academic, must be measured *in time intervals.* Records must be kept which are precise and accurate.

Behavior — The contingent result of <u>Life.</u>

Behaviors are learned in time through contingent reinforcement. Therefore the teacher must structure the student's life experiences if effective learning is to take place. How much control is to be exercised depends upon the values of the teacher. *Reinforcement teaching is the structure of approval and disapproval responses, in time, to shape desired behavior toward specific goals.* Deviant behavior is often eliminated by cutting out the payoff; wholesome learning is established by instituting a payoff. The teacher must observe the student closely—paying particular attention to what happens immediately before and after a specified behavior—to become proficient in behavioral analysis. It should be remembered that when the teacher begins to structure or restructure environmental contingencies, problems of "fairness" arise. The teacher then must discriminate between many separate and related social and/or academic issues to decide what is to be done, i.e., what's fair. Approval-disapproval techniques for shaping desired behavior include every available personal response as well as all objects at the teacher's disposal: subject matter, words, expressions, closeness, activities and things. Personal responses should be overtly practiced. Merely reading, discussing, and thinking about responses is not enough to develop these tools effectively.

Life—The structure of activities in <u>Time</u>

Everything happens in time; indeed, *life is time.* Temporal aspects of life are not only extremely important but highly elusive as well. Therefore, precise timing in delivering responses cannot be overemphasized. While temporal consistency is the single most important aspect of discipline, it is also the most difficult. In order to discipline effectively, the teacher must structure everything *in time.* Structural manipulation of the external environment is based upon these steps: (1) *Pinpoint*— defining the *problem* behavior to be eliminated, the *new behavior* to be learned or both (teaching incompatible responses). Pinpointing regarding *subject matter* is accomplished by structuring specific measurable goals; pinpointing *maladaptive social responses* necessitates defining deviant responses specifically in overt categories and observing the child carefully. These observations not only establish what stimuli are presently reinforcing undesired behavior but also provide clues for selecting effective reinforcers which can be used to establish other responses. (2) *Record*—assessing behavior quantitatively. It is imperative that accurate records be kept. Otherwise the teacher can never ascertain the relationship between the frequency and magnitude of the *old* social/academic adaptive/deviant behaviors and the new. Records must be precise and recordings must be done *in time intervals*. (3) *Consequate*—controlling the external environment through the use of approval-disapproval reinforcers delivered contingently on time schedules to teach desired behaviors. (4) *Evaluate*—measuring the frequency of behavior to see if the behavior gets better or worse. Most often, thoughtfully prescribed contingencies decrease objectional behaviors from the original recorded level and/or increase desirable responses. If selected reinforcers are not effective, a new structure may be required and other contingencies established. Indeed, restructuring regarding all aspects of instruction should represent a continuous process toward greater refinement and increased teaching effectiveness.

Effective teaching takes much practice. Similar to other pursuits in life, the rewards of teaching seem both proportional to, and contingent upon, thoughtful involvement, structured action, and continuous learning and evaluation. Hopefully, the end product of this teaching will be a person who is informed, who is individually productive and socially responsible, who has the ability to analyze, criticize, and choose alternatives, and who has a compelling system of values whereby he may actualize his life in a manner consistent with ever-increasing knowledge— in a word, a person who evidences **discipline**.

ADDENDUM

The authors are dedicated both in practice and research to the improvement of education at all levels and in all specialties. Thus, we share some of the same values expressed by teachers in many divergent programs throughout teaching and related professions. Most of the specific techniques and principles found in this book came from teachers—beginning teachers, special education teachers, elementary, secondary, vocational-technical, and college teachers; teachers for gifted, for emotionally disturbed, for physically handicapped, and for children with learning disabilities; art, music, speech and hearing, home economics, and physical education teachers; content area specialists, subject matter specialists, and resource specialists; preschool, child development, and nursery school teachers; social workers, counselors, and school psychologists; more especially *older teachers* whose long-term experiences have too long been ignored or repudiated by those very students who through scholarly denunciation attest to the effectiveness of their past learning.

In a continuing effort to learn of effective and ineffective practices in teaching, the authors sincerely encourage written responses from teachers. We would like information concerning techniques, materials, special projects, and any conceivable procedure used in teaching social and/or academic behaviors. Written responses will be used toward the goal of improving education through research, application, and continuous dissemination. Teachers who share this concern please send responses to:

Madsen & Madsen
Teaching/Discipline
Allyn and Bacon
470 Atlantic Avenue
Boston, Mass. 02210

REFERENCES FOR
SCIENTIFIC APPLICATIONS

1. S.G. Doubros and C.J. Daniels, "An Experimental Approach to the Reduction of Overactive Behavior," *Behavior Research and Therapy,* 1966, *4,* 251-258.
2. C.B. Ferster, "Arithmetic Behavior in Chimpanzees," *Scientific American,* 1964, *210,* 2-9.
3. W.C. Becker, C.H. Madsen, Jr., C.R. Arnold, and D.R. Thomas, "The Contingent Use of Teacher Attention and Praise in Reducing Classroom Problems," *Journal of Special Education,* 1967, *1,* 287-307.
4. P.E. Baer and G. Goldfarb, "A Developmental Study of Verbal Conditioning in Children," *Psychological Reports,* 1962, *10,* 175-181.
5. D.S. Holms, "The Application of Learning Theory to the Treatment of a School Behavior Problem: A Case Study," *Psychology in the Schools,* 1966, *3,* 355-359.
6. A.T. Jersild and F.B. Holmes, "Methods of Overcoming Children's Fears," *Journal of Psychology,* 1935, *1,* 75-104.
7. R.V. Hall, D. Lund, and D. Jackson, "Effects of Teacher Attention on Study Behavior," *Journal of Applied Behavior Analysis,* 1968, *1,* 1-12.
8. F.R. Harris, M. Johnston, S. Kelley, and M.M. Wolf, "Effects of Positive Social Reinforcement on Regressed Crawling of a Nursery School Child," *Journal of Educational Psychology,* 1964, *55,* 35-41.
9. K. Miller, "A Note on the Control of Study Behavior," *Journal of Experimental Child Psychology,* 1965, *1,* 108-110.
10. P. Brown and R. Elliott, "Control of Aggression in a Nursery School Class," *Journal of Experimental Child Psychology,* 1965, *2,* 103-107.
11. K.E. Allen, B.M. Hart, J.S. Buell, F.R. Harris, and M.M. Wolf, "Effects of Social Reinforcement on Isolate Behavior of a Nursery School Child," *Child Development,* 1964, *35,* 511-518.
12. K.D. O'Leary and W.C. Becker, "Behavior Modification of an Adjustment Class: A Token Reinforcement Program," *Exceptional Children,* 1967, *9,* 637-642.

13. R.R. Martin and G.M. Siegel, "The Effects of Response Contingent Shock on Stuttering," *Journal of Speech and Hearing Research,* 1966, *9,* 340-352.
14. C.H. Madsen, Jr., W.C. Becker, D. R. Thomas, and E. Plager, "An Analysis of the Reinforcing Functions of 'Sit-down' Commands," in *Readings in Educational Psychology,* ed. R.K. Parker (Boston: Allyn and Bacon, Inc., 1968).
15. K.D. O'Leary and W.C. Becker, "The Effects of the Intensity of a Teacher's Reprimands on Children's Behavior," *Journal of School Psychology,* 1968, *7,* 8-11.
16. G.R. Patterson, "An Application of Conditioning Techniques to the Control of a Hyperactive Child," in *Case Studies in Behavior Modification,* ed. L.P. Ullmann and L. Krasner (New York: Holt, Rinehart, and Winston, 1965).
17. D.G. Ellson, L. Barber, T.L. Engle, and L. Kampwerth, "Programmed Tutoring: A Teaching Aid and Research Tool," *Reading Research Quarterly,* 1965, *1,* 77-127.
18. R.P. Hawkins, R.F. Peterson, E. Schweid, and S.W. Bijou, "Behavior Therapy in the Home: Amelioration of Problem Parent-Child Relations with the Parent in a Therapeutic Role," *Journal of Experimental Child Psychology,* 1966, *4,* 99-107.
19. R.V. Hall, M. Panyan, D. Rabon, and M. Broden, "Instructing Beginning Teachers in Reinforcement Procedures Which Improve Classroom Control," *Journal of Applied Behavior Analysis,* 1968, *1,* 315-328.
20. C.H. Madsen, Jr., W.C. Becker, and D.R. Thomas, "Rules, Praise, and Ignoring: Elements of Elementary Classroom Control," *Journal of Applied Behavior Analysis,* 1968, *1,* 139-150.
21. R. Schwitzgebel and D.A. Kolb, "Inducing Behavior Changes in Adolescent Delinquents," *Behavior Research and Therapy,* 1964, *1,* 297-304.
22. R.J. Wahler, G.H. Winkel, R.E. Peterson, and D.C. Morrison, "Mothers as Behavior Therapists for Their Own Children," *Behavior Research and Therapy,* 1965, *3,* 113-124.